Essential Preparation for

UMAT

UNDERGRADUATE MEDICINE & HEALTH SCIENCES ADMISSION TEST

Series Two

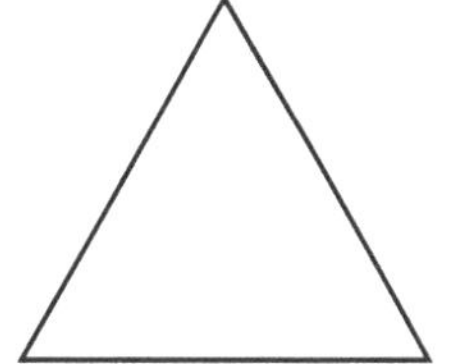

BOOK 3
NON-VERBAL REASONING

Mohan Dhall

Five Senses Education Pty Ltd
2/195 Prospect Highway
Seven Hills 2147
New South Wales
Australia

First Published 2013

Dhall, Mohan
Series 2, Book 3 - Non-Verbal Reasoning

ISBN 978-1-74130-894-5

CONTENTS

UMAT Trial Examination

Total Test Time: 180 minutes

- **Section 1: 48 Questions (70 minutes)**
- **Section 2: 44 Questions (55 minutes)**
- **Section 3: 42 Questions (55 minutes)**

This book covers Section 3

Section 3 – Non-Verbal Reasoning (55 minutes)

Questions in this section may be of several kinds. All are based on patterns or sequences of shapes and are designed to assess your ability to reason in the abstract and to solve problems in non-verbal contexts.

Section 3 - Non Verbal Reasoning

Question 1

Select the alternative that most logically and simply continues the series.

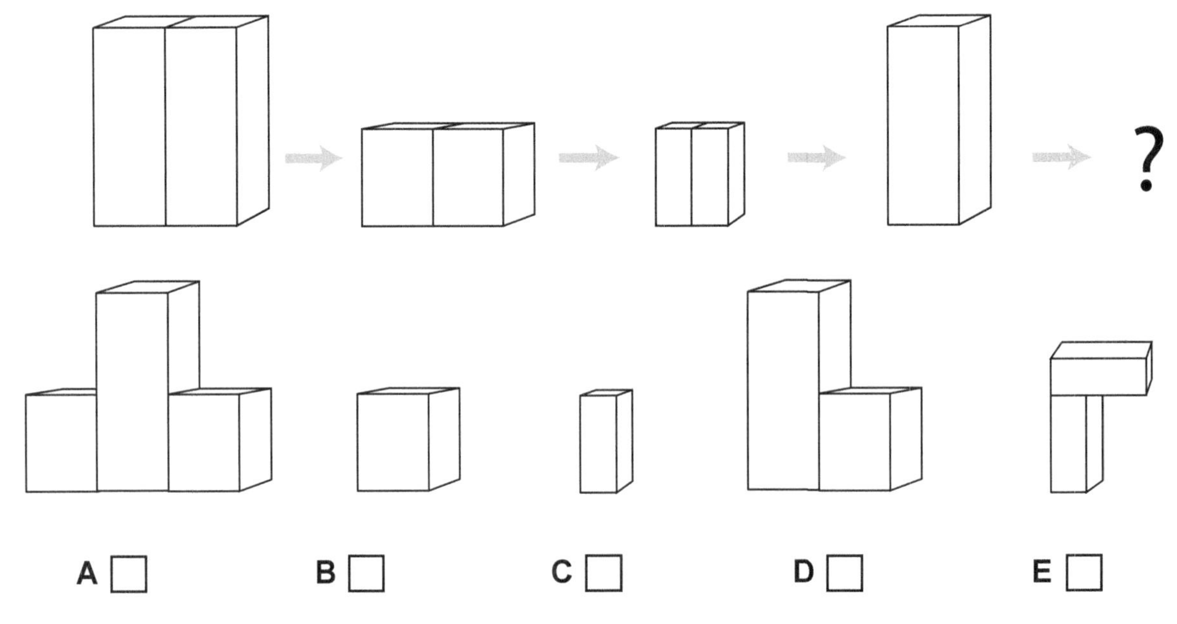

Question 2

Select the alternative that most logically and simply continues the series.

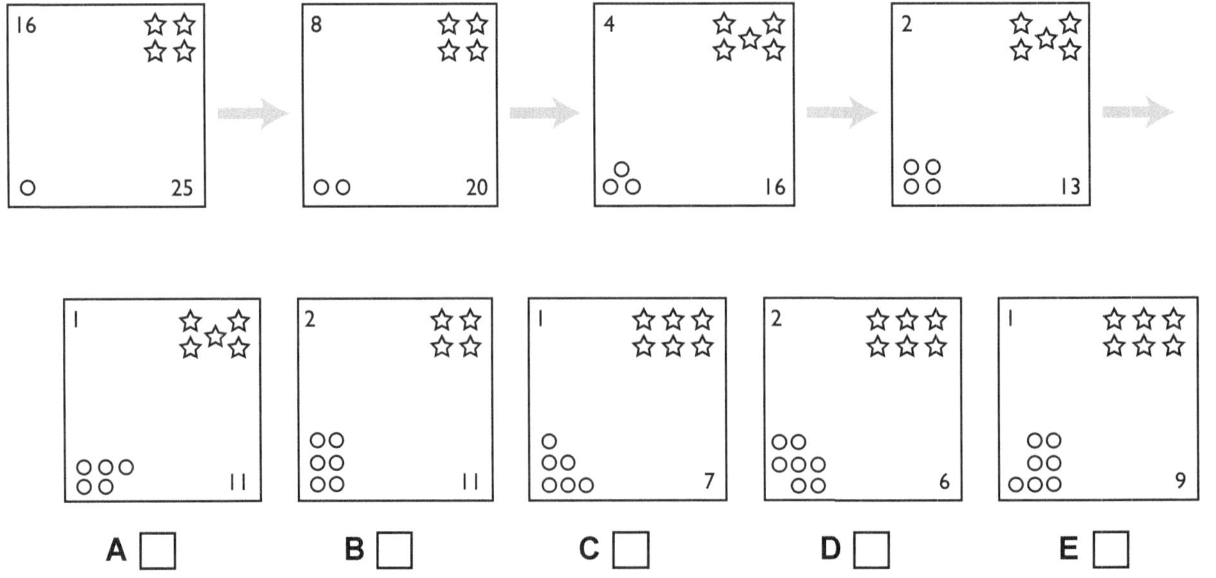

Section 3 - Non Verbal Reasoning

Question 3

Select the alternative that most logically and simply continues the series.

AZK → BAJ → BYH → CZK → ?

CXL DAL CXE DYL CAD

A ☐ B ☐ C ☐ D ☐ E ☐

Question 4

Select the alternative that most logically and simply continues the series.

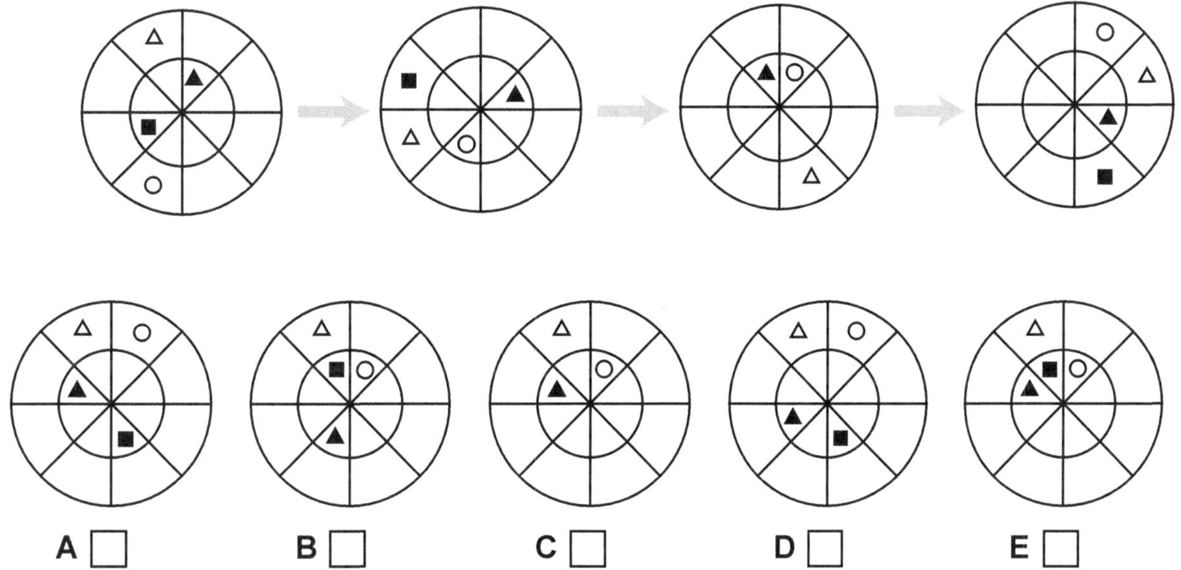

Section 3 - Non Verbal Reasoning

Question 5

Select the alternative that most logically and simply continues the series.

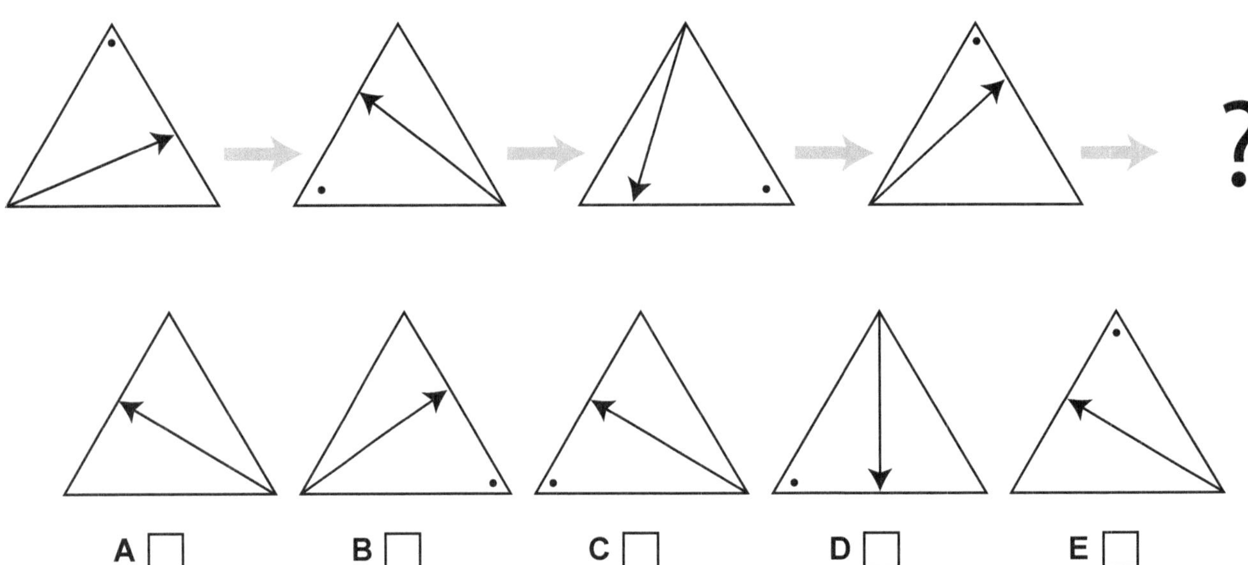

Section 3 - Non Verbal Reasoning

Question 6

Select the alternative that most logically and simply continues the series.

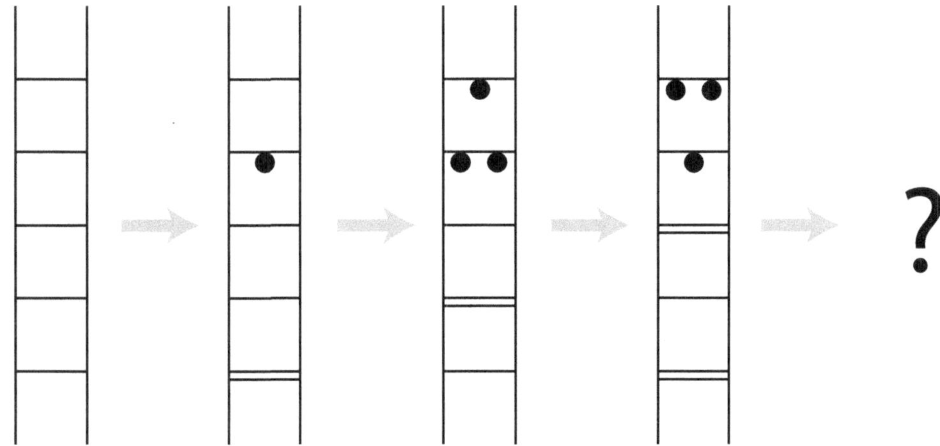

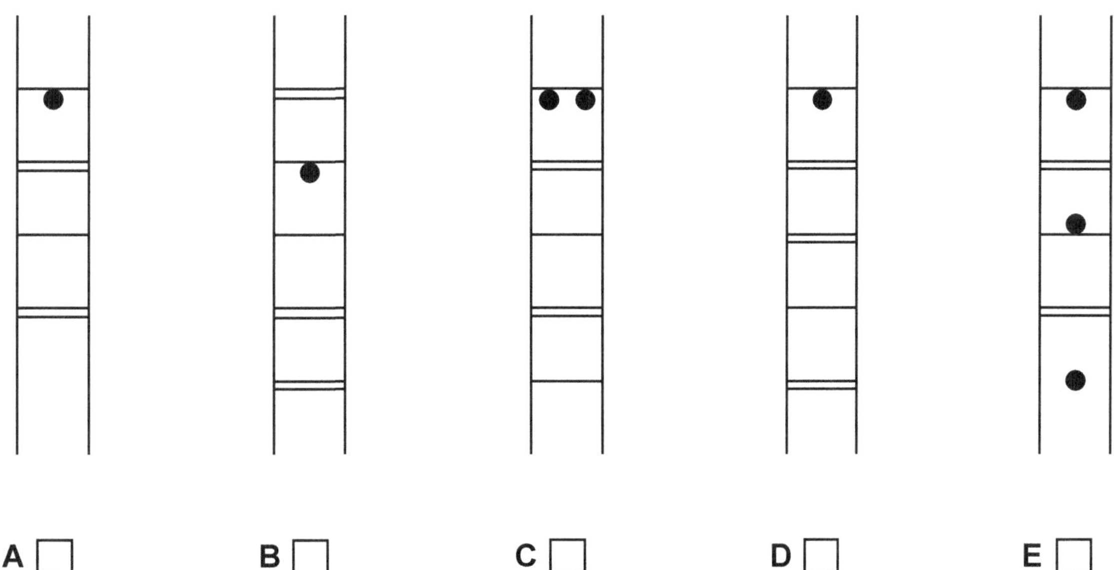

A ☐ B ☐ C ☐ D ☐ E ☐

Section 3 - Non Verbal Reasoning

Question 7

Select the alternative that most logically and simply continues the series.

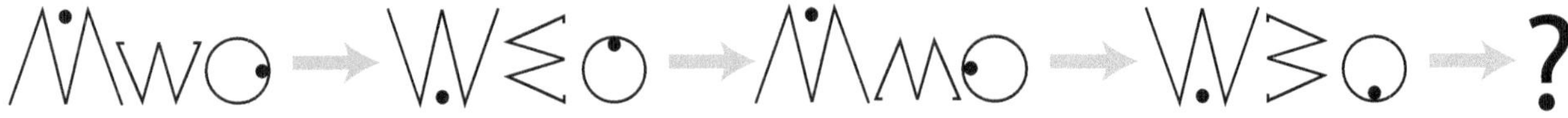

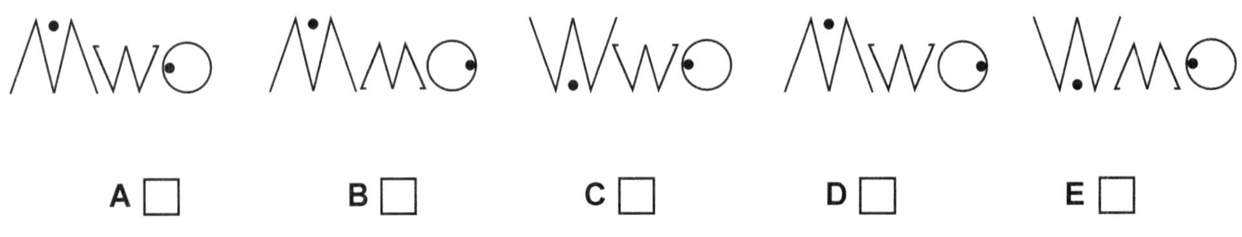

A ☐ B ☐ C ☐ D ☐ E ☐

Question 8

Select the alternative that most logically and simply continues the series.

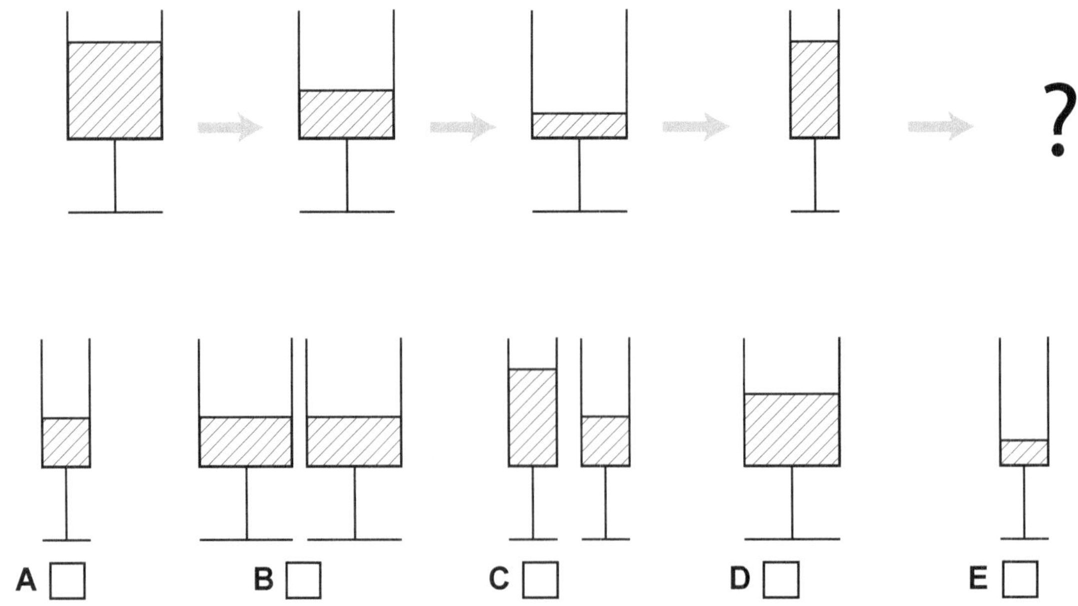

A ☐ B ☐ C ☐ D ☐ E ☐

Section 3 - Non Verbal Reasoning

Question 9

Select the alternative that most logically and simply continues the series.

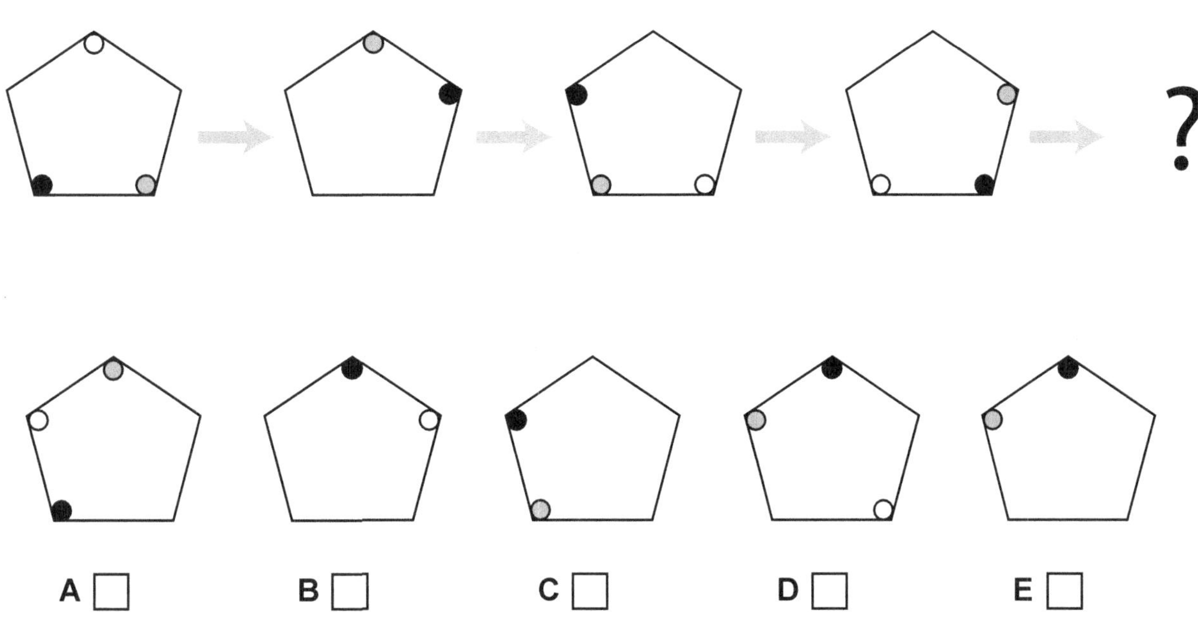

Question 10

Select the alternative that most logically and simply continues the series.

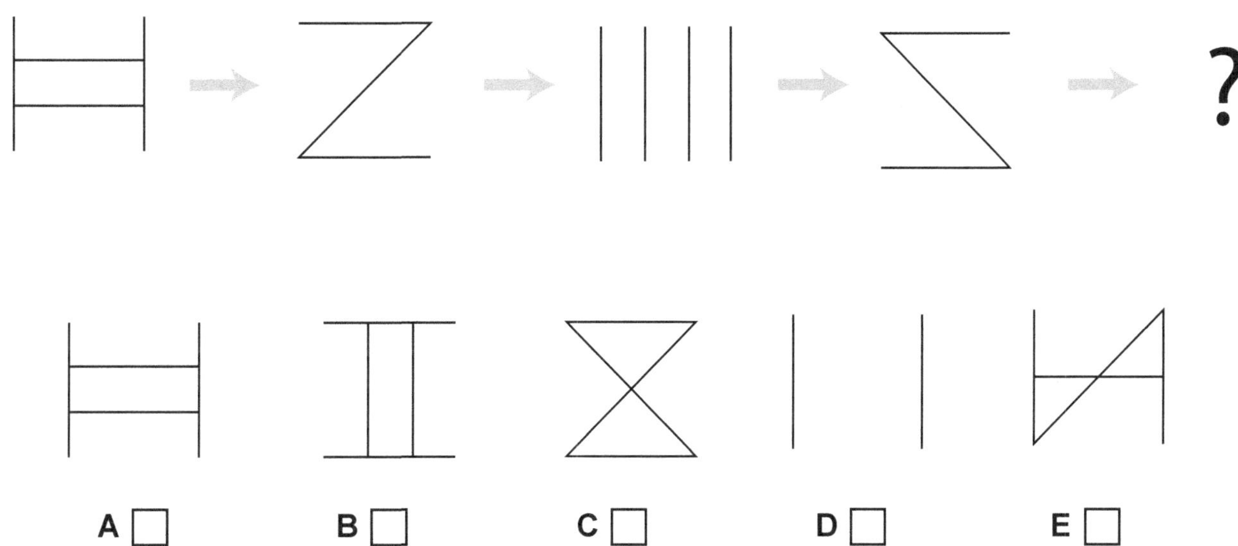

Section 3 - Non Verbal Reasoning

Question 11

Select the alternative that most logically and simply continues the series.

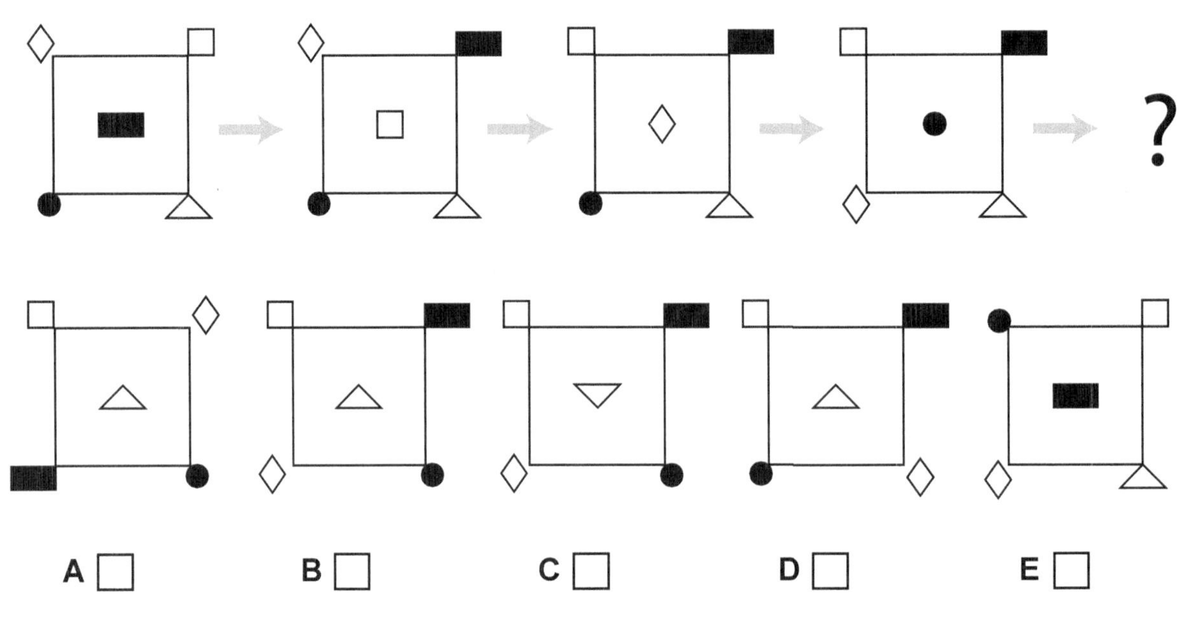

A ☐ B ☐ C ☐ D ☐ E ☐

Question 12

Select the alternative that most logically and simply continues the series.

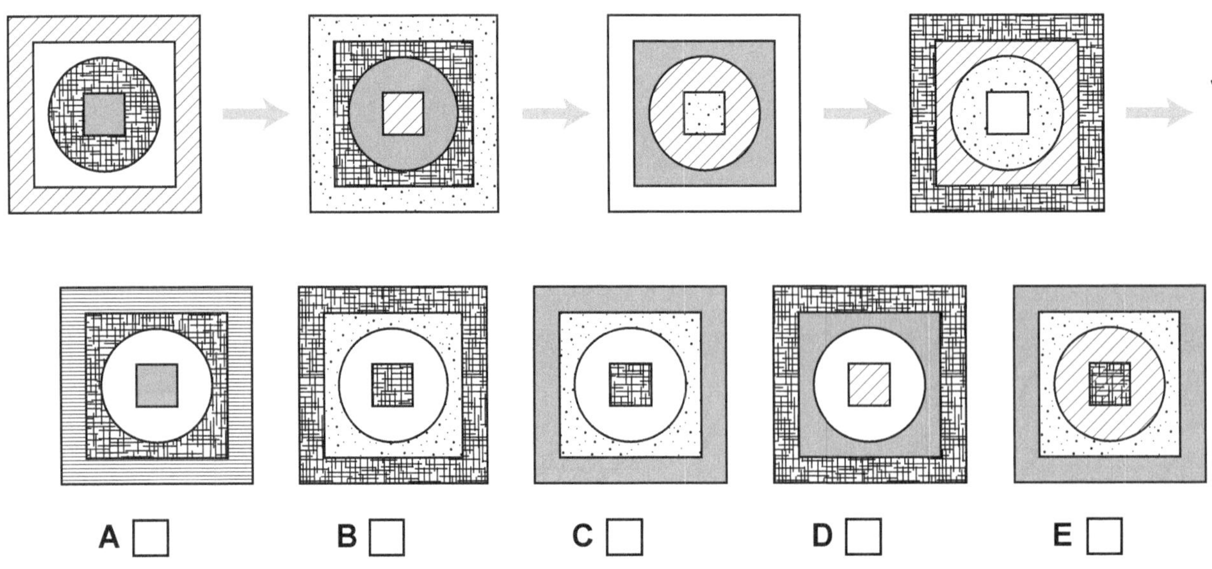

A ☐ B ☐ C ☐ D ☐ E ☐

Section 3 - Non Verbal Reasoning

Question 13

Select the alternative that most logically and simply continues the series.

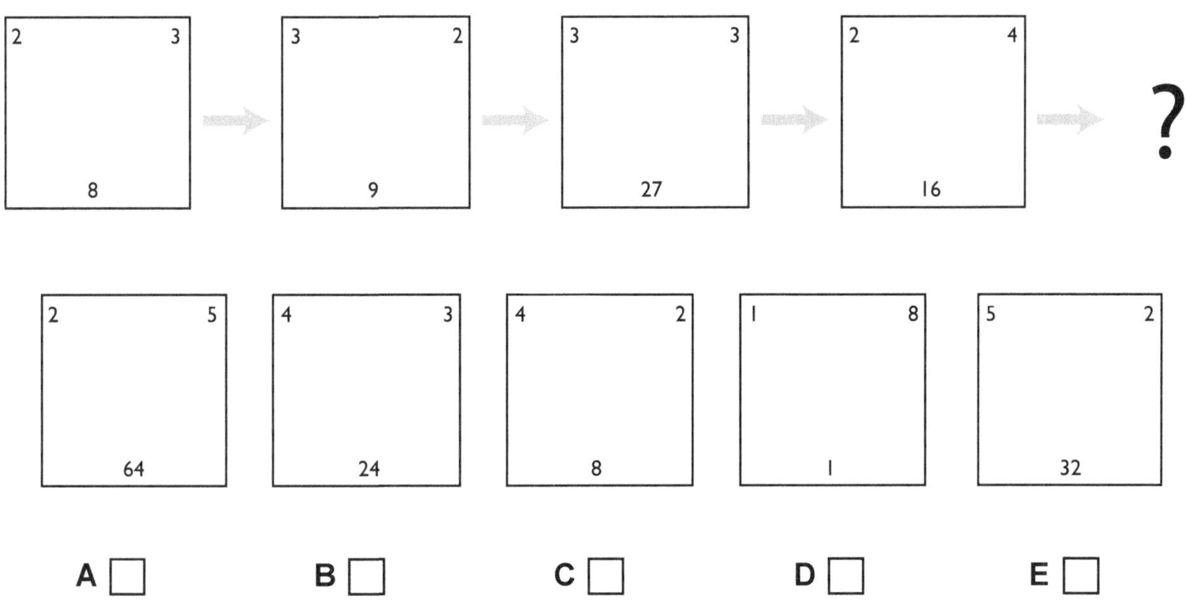

A ☐ B ☐ C ☐ D ☐ E ☐

Question 14

Select the alternative that most logically and simply continues the series.

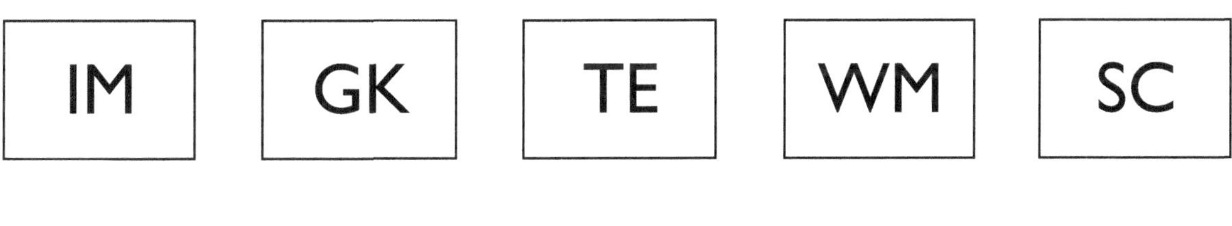

IM	GK	TE	WM	SC

A ☐ B ☐ C ☐ D ☐ E ☐

Section 3 - Non Verbal Reasoning

Question 15

Select the alternative that most logically and simply completes the picture.

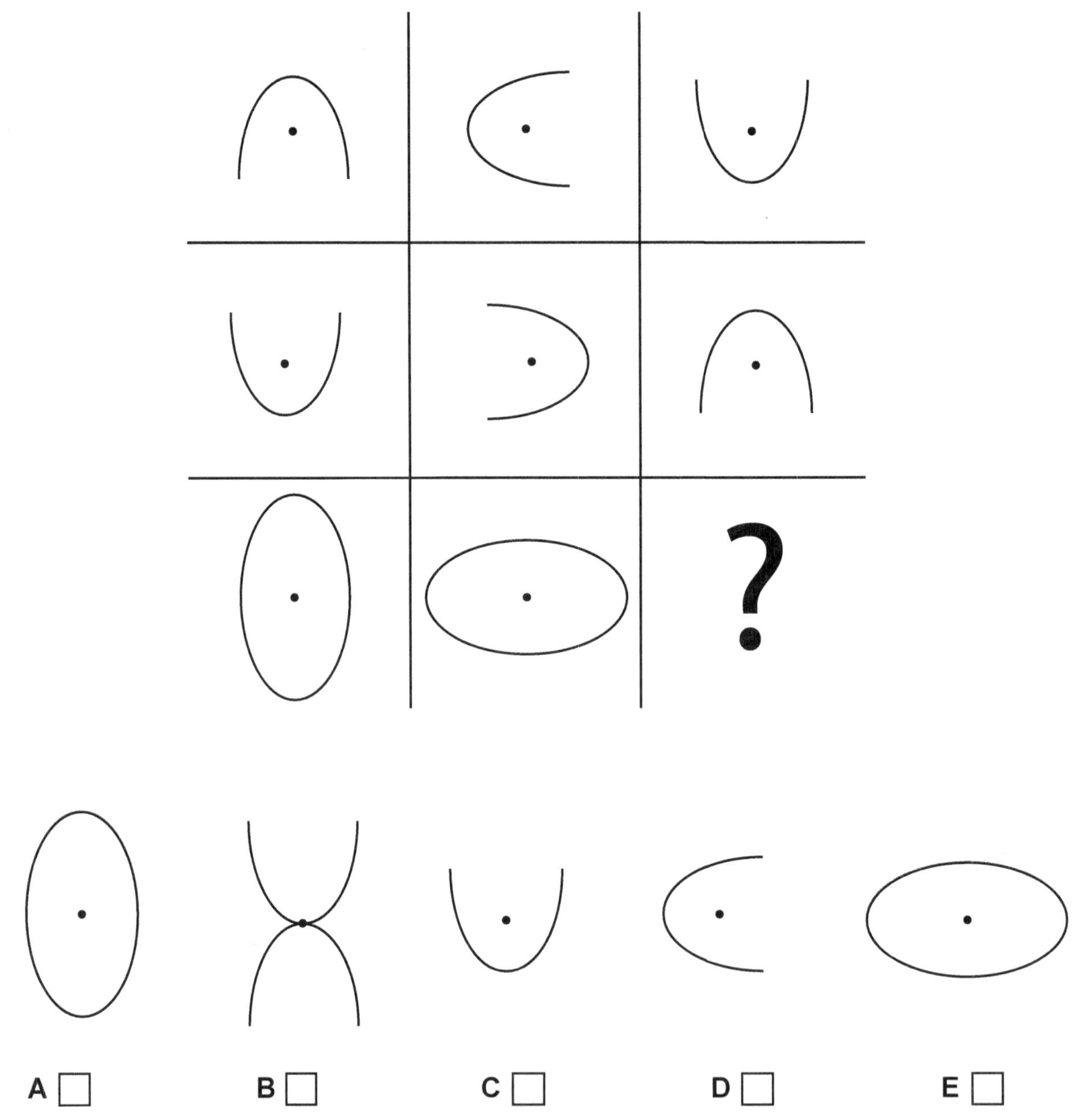

Section 3 - Non Verbal Reasoning

Question 16

Select the alternative that most logically and simply completes the picture.

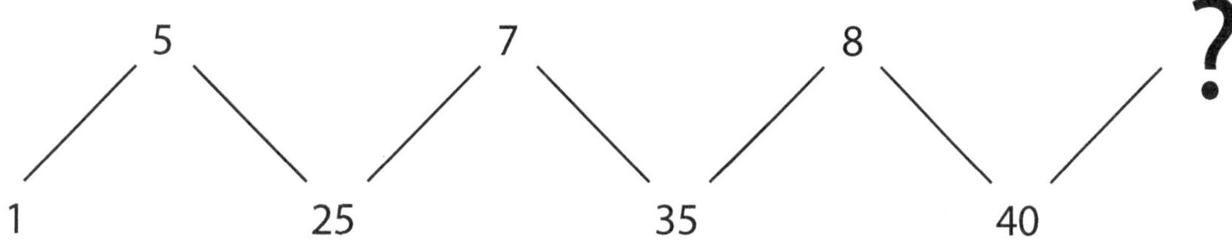

10	9	40	4	3
A ☐	B ☐	C ☐	D ☐	E ☐

Section 3 - Non Verbal Reasoning

Question 17

Select the alternative that most logically and simply completes the picture.

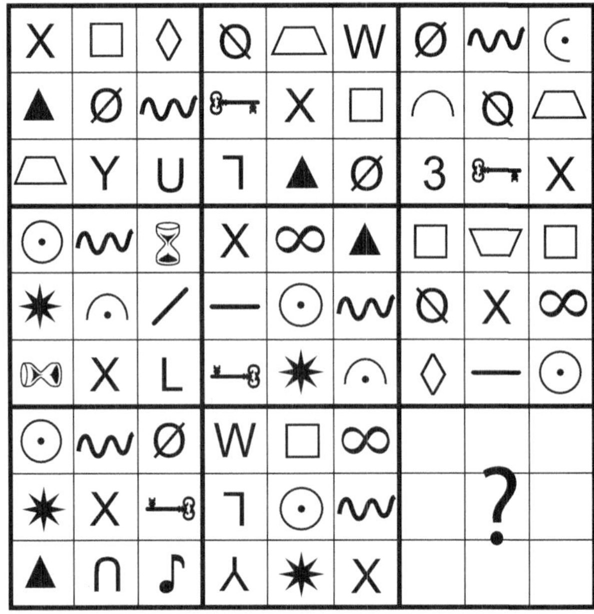

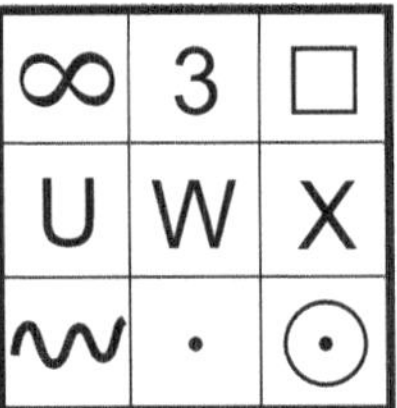

A

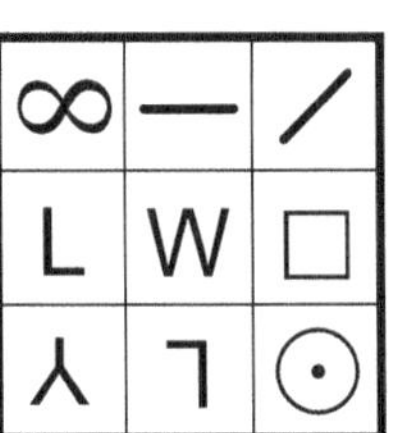

B

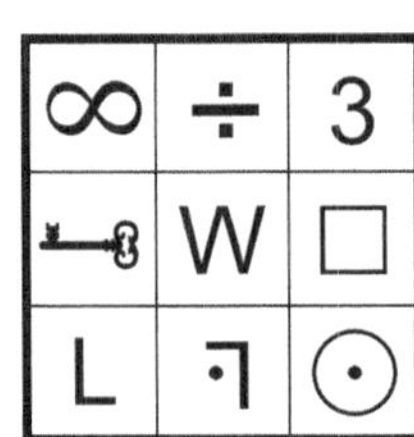

C

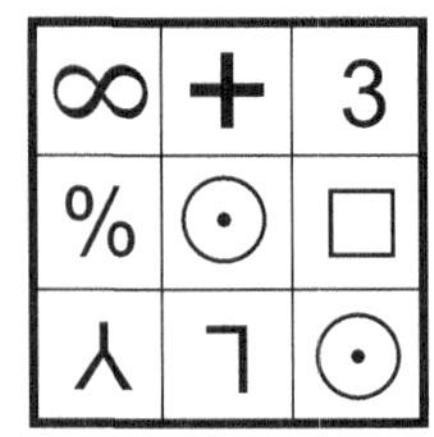

D

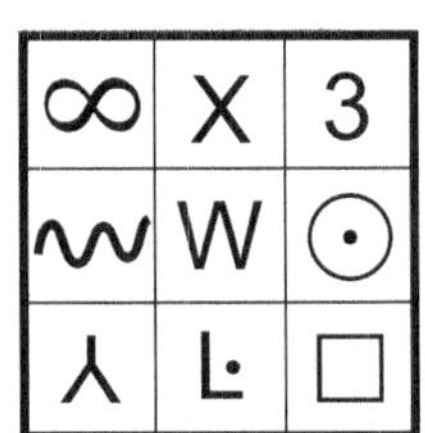

E

Section 3 - Non Verbal Reasoning

Question 18

Select the alternative that most logically and simply completes the picture.

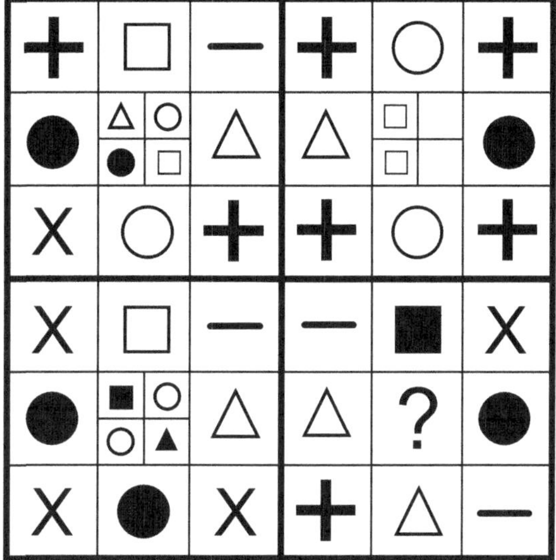

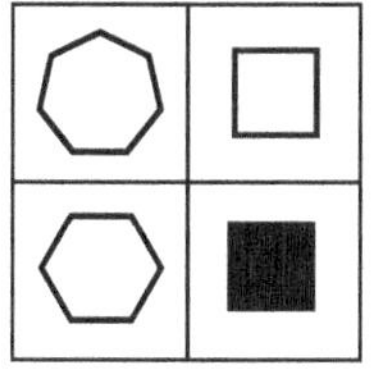

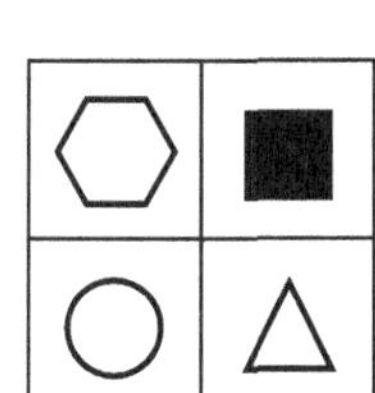

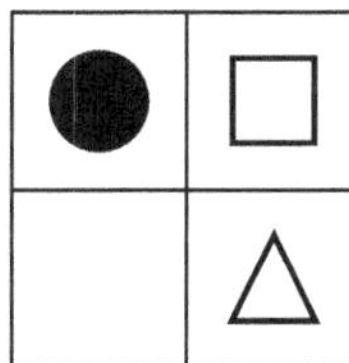

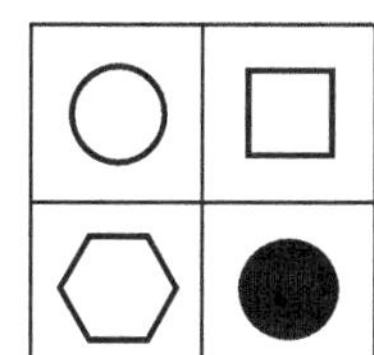

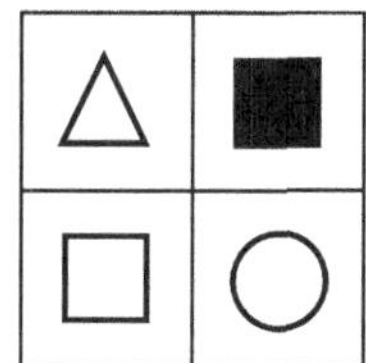

A ☐ B ☐ C ☐ D ☐ E ☐

Section 3 - Non Verbal Reasoning

Question 19

Select the alternative that most logically and simply completes the picture.

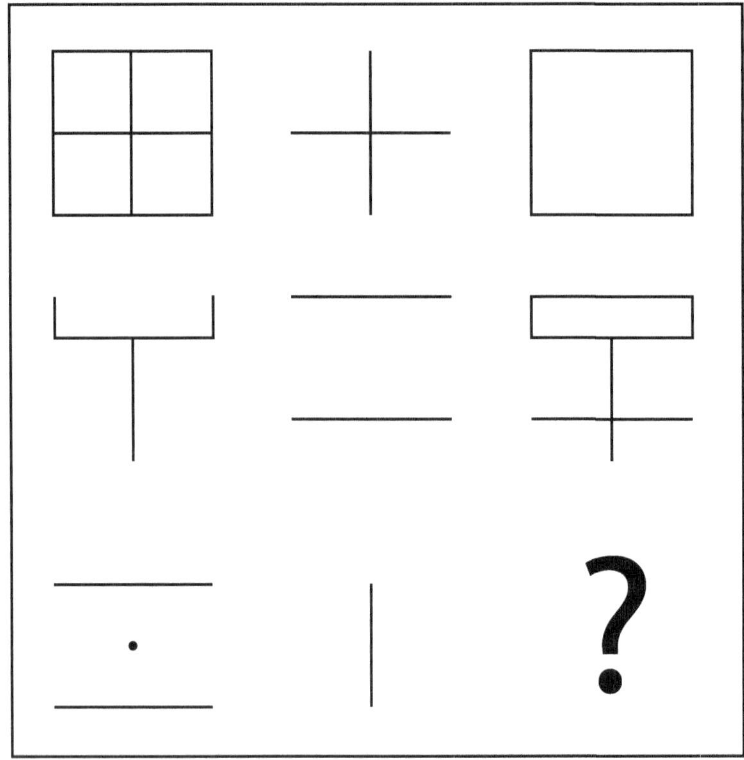

A ☐ B ☐ C ☐ D ☐ E ☐

Section 3 - Non Verbal Reasoning

Question 20

Select the alternative that most logically and simply completes the picture.

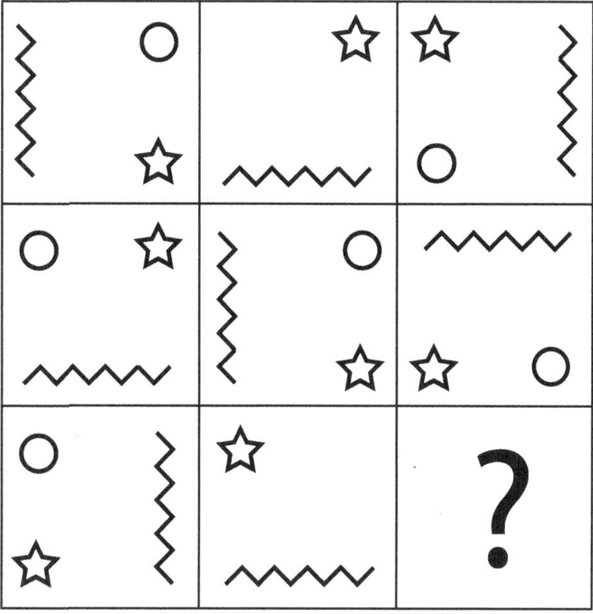

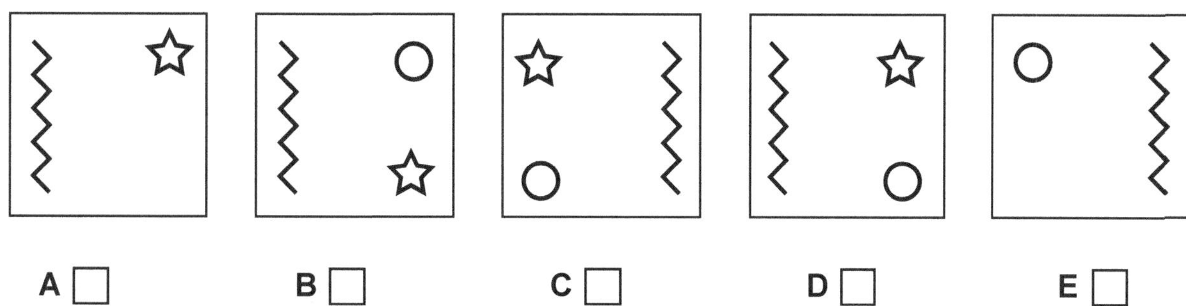

A ☐ B ☐ C ☐ D ☐ E ☐

Section 3 - Non Verbal Reasoning

Question 21

Select the alternative that most logically and simply completes the picture.

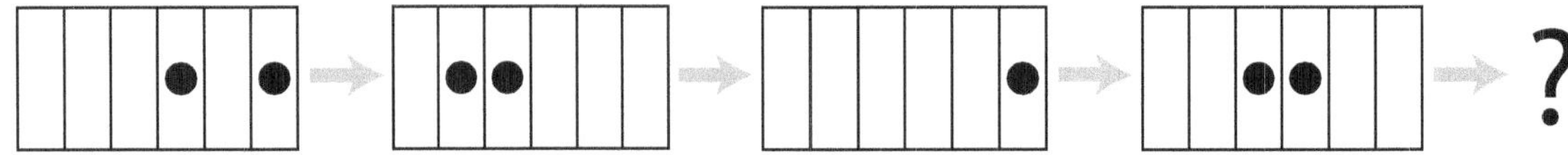

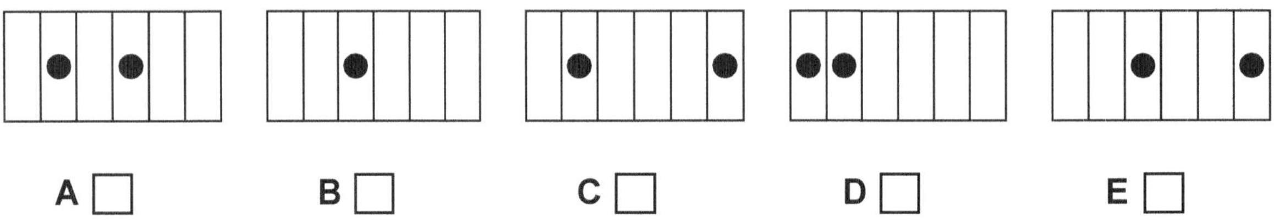

A ☐ B ☐ C ☐ D ☐ E ☐

Question 22

Select the alternative that most logically and simply completes the picture.

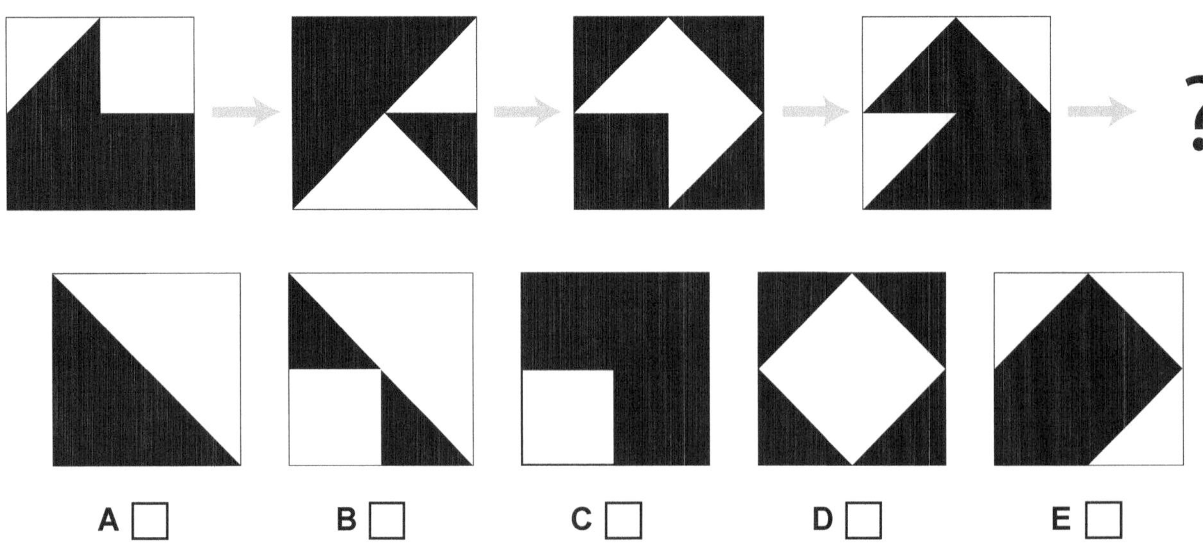

A ☐ B ☐ C ☐ D ☐ E ☐

Section 3 - Non Verbal Reasoning

Question 23

Select the alternative that most logically and simply completes the picture.

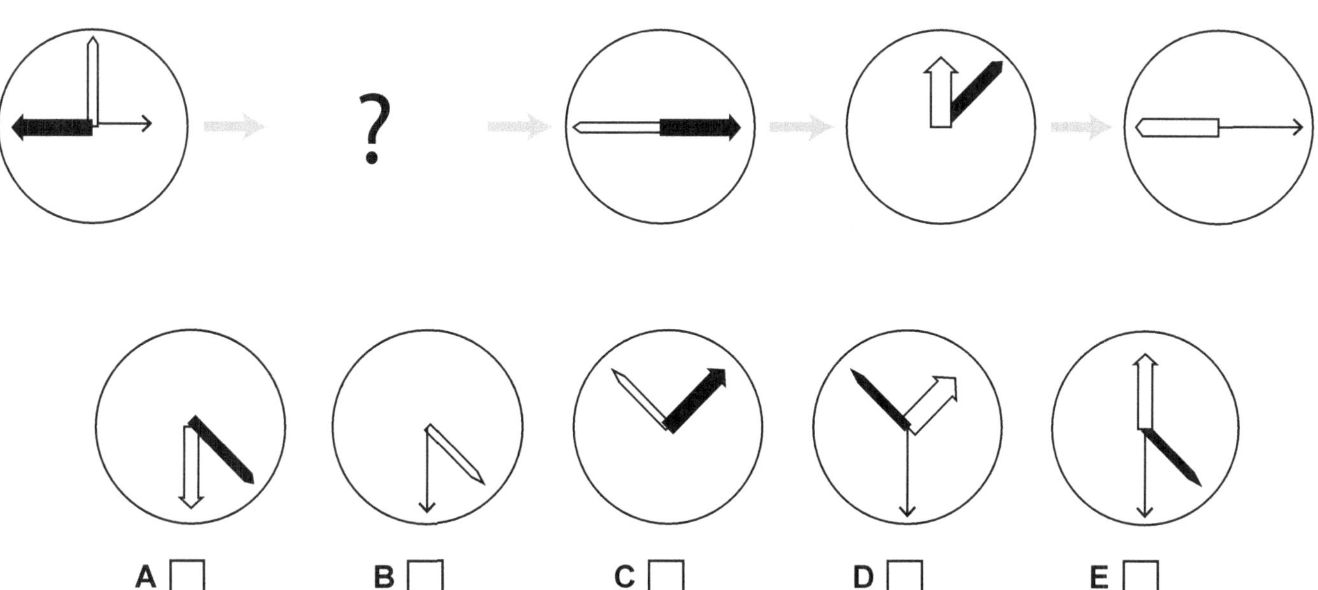

Section 3 - Non Verbal Reasoning

Question 24

Select the alternative that most logically and simply completes the picture.

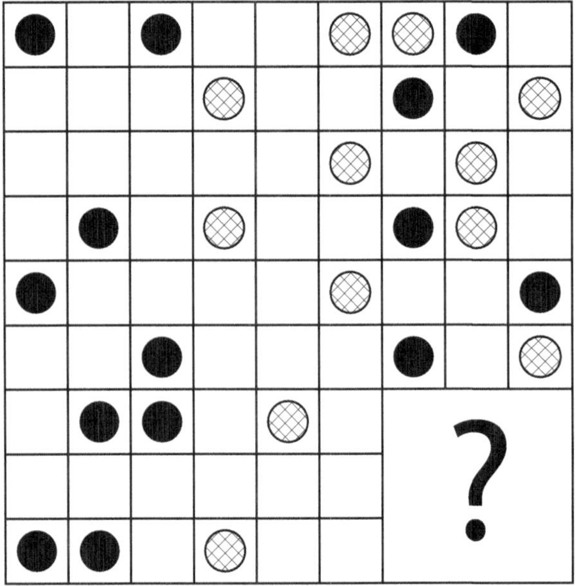

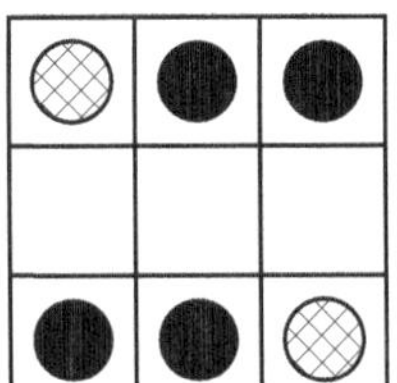

A

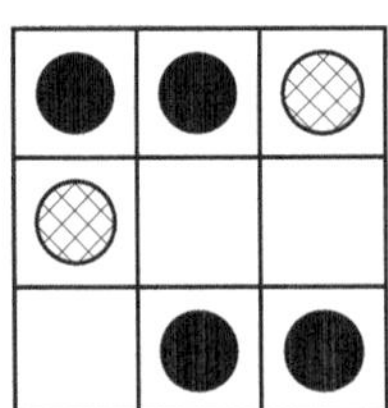

B

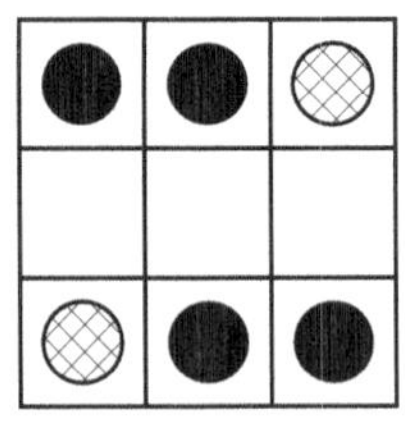

C

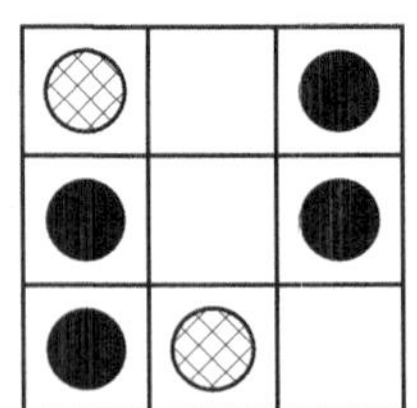

D

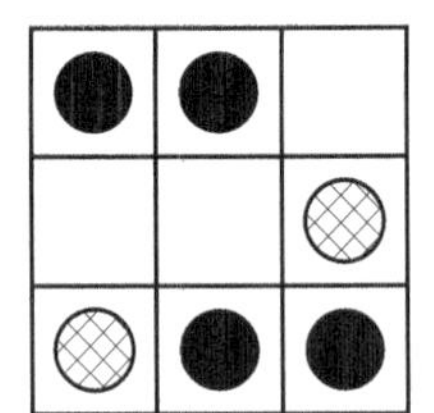

E

Section 3 - Non Verbal Reasoning

Question 25

Select the alternative that most logically and simply completes the picture.

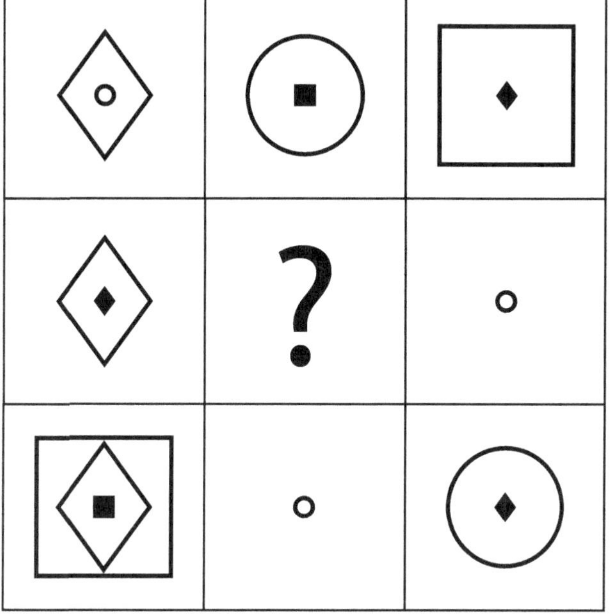

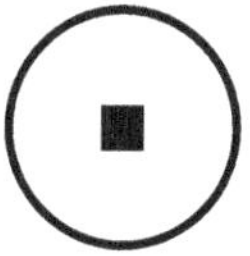

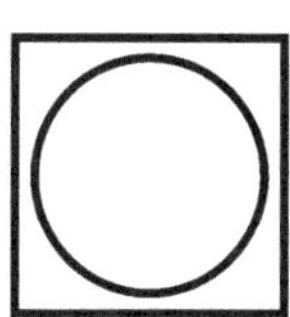

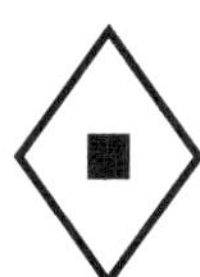

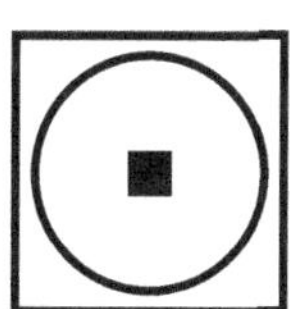

A ☐ B ☐ C ☐ D ☐ E ☐

Section 3 - Non Verbal Reasoning

Question 26

Select the alternative that most logically and simply completes the picture.

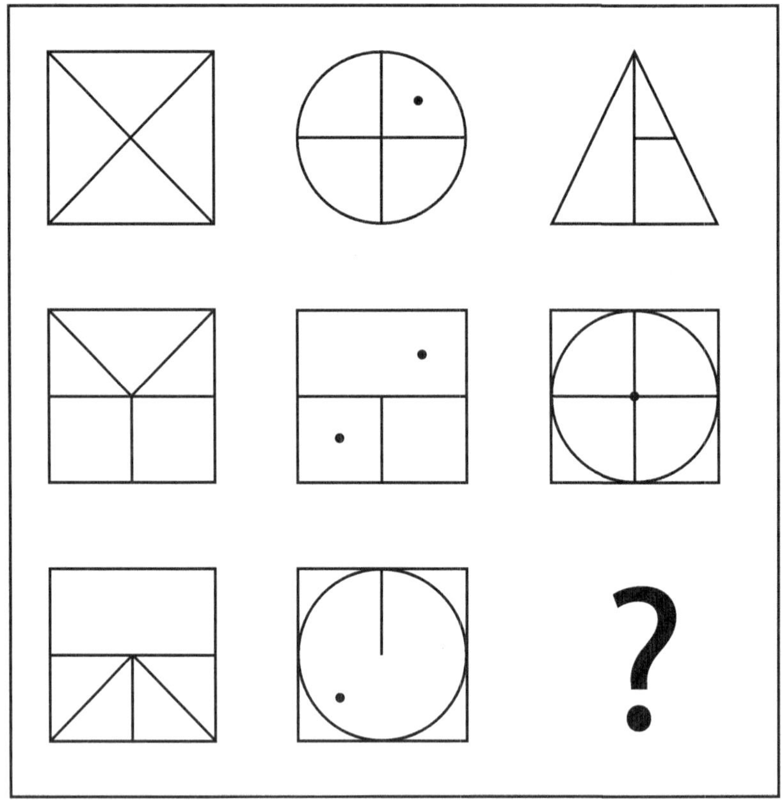

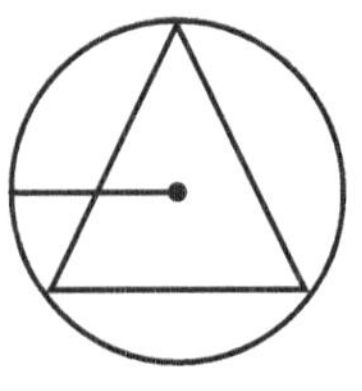

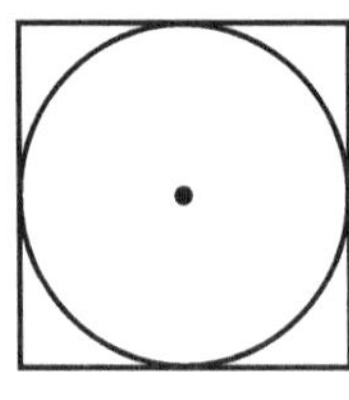

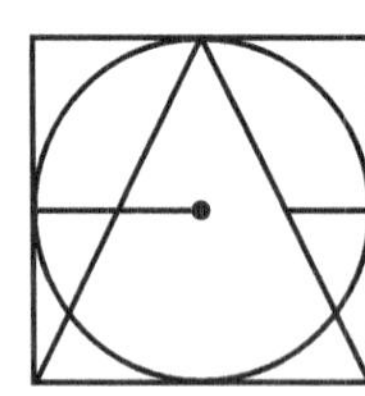

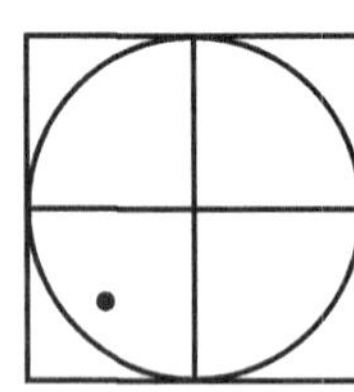

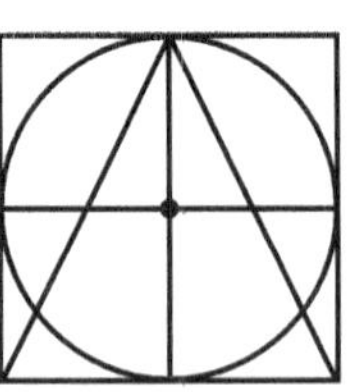

A ☐ B ☐ C ☐ D ☐ E ☐

Section 3 - Non Verbal Reasoning

Question 27

Select the alternative that most logically and simply completes the picture.

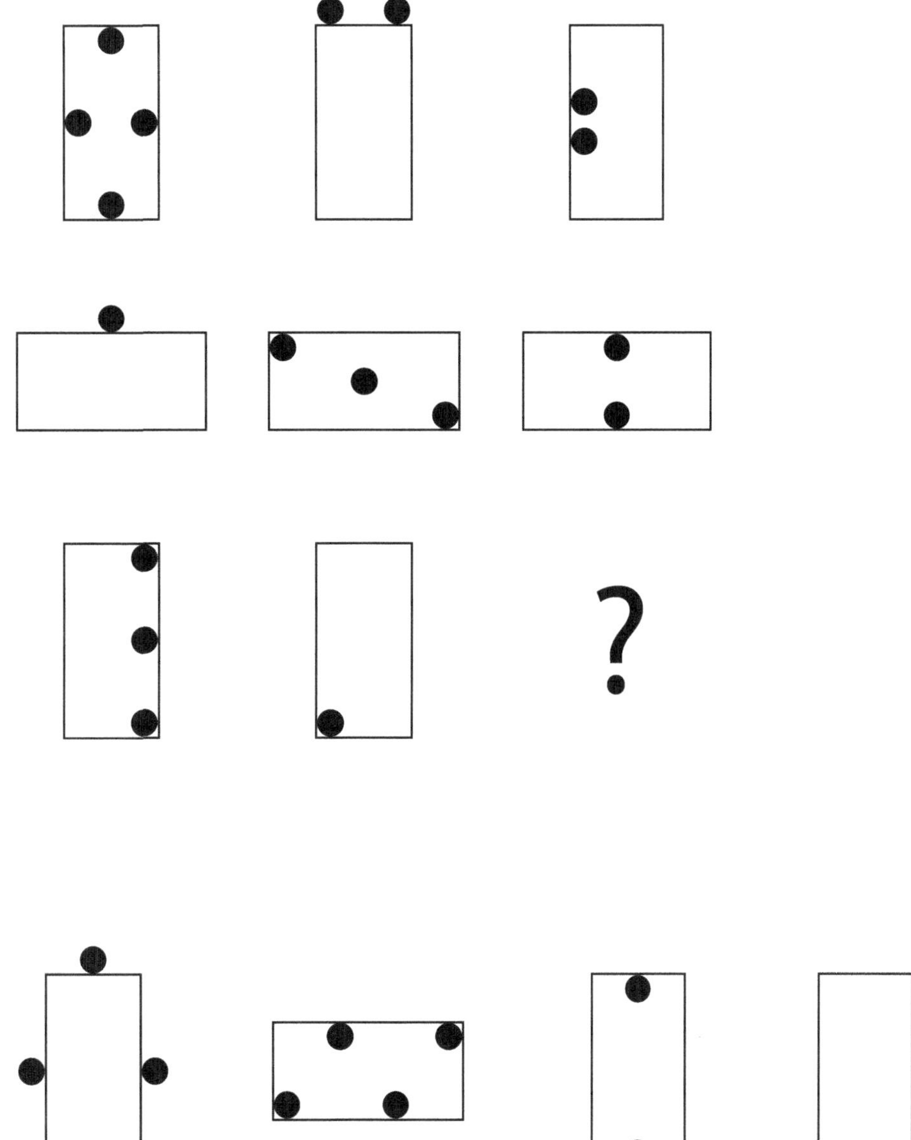

A ☐ B ☐ C ☐ D ☐ E ☐

Section 3 - Non Verbal Reasoning

Question 28

Select the alternative that most logically and simply completes the picture.

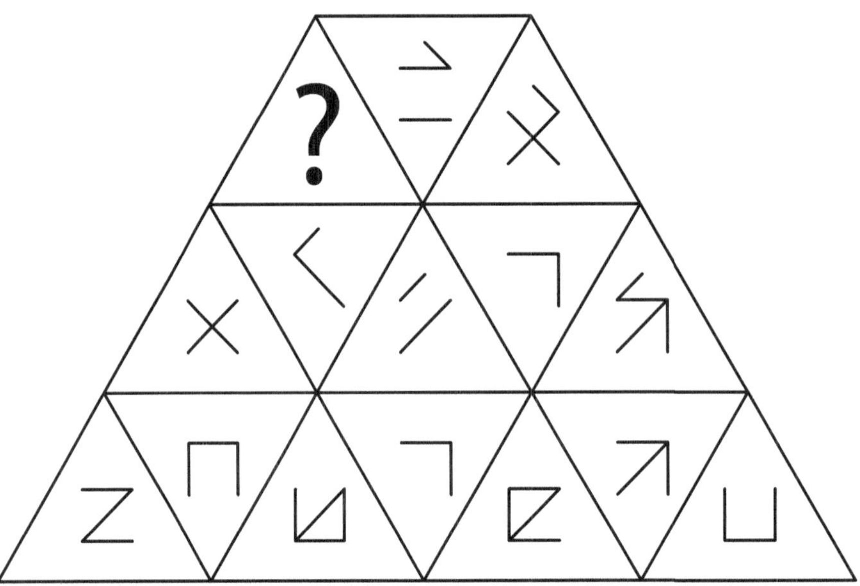

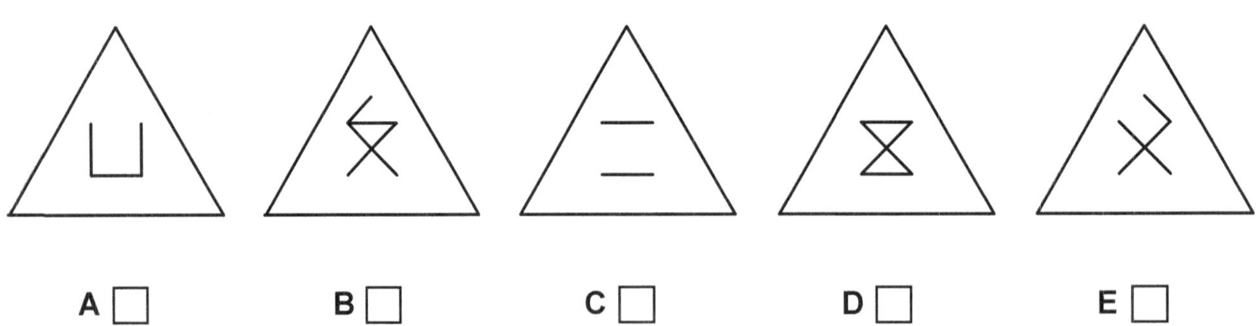

A ☐ B ☐ C ☐ D ☐ E ☐

Section 3 - Non Verbal Reasoning

Question 29

In the questions below, the five figures can be rearranged to form a logical sequence.
Select the alternative that would most logically and simply be in the <u>middle</u> of the sequence.

PQUVB	PQUUA	PQBVB	PQUVA	OQUUA

A ☐ B ☐ C ☐ D ☐ E ☐

Question 30

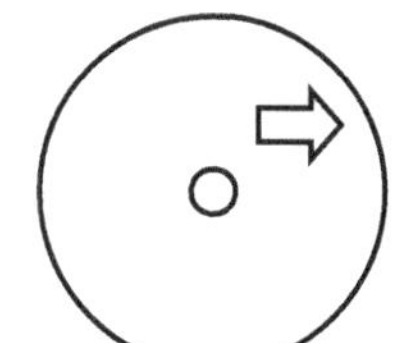
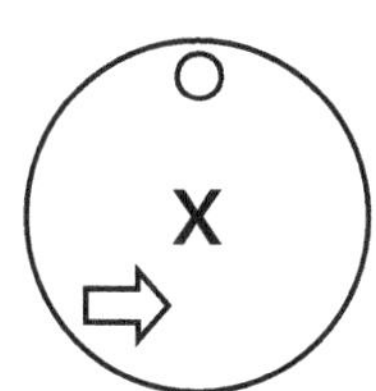

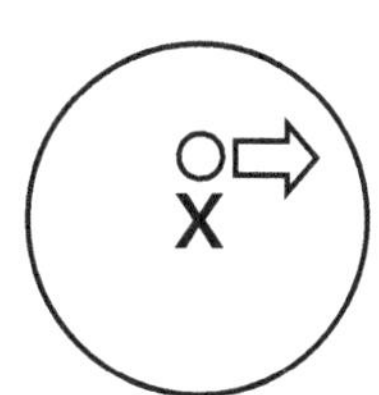

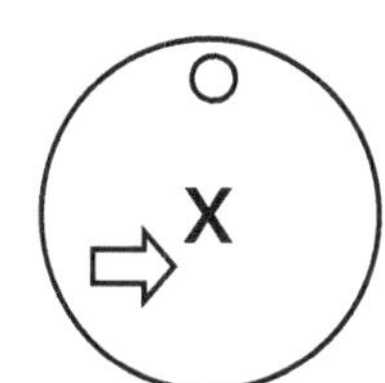

A ☐ B ☐ C ☐ D ☐ E ☐

Section 3 - Non Verbal Reasoning

In the questions below, the five figures can be rearranged to form a logical sequence.
Select the alternative that would most logically and simply be in the <u>middle</u> of the sequence.

Question 31

A ☐ B ☐ C ☐ D ☐ E ☐

Question 32

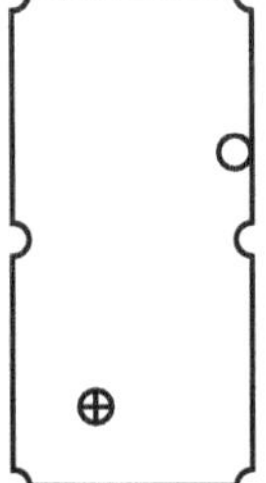
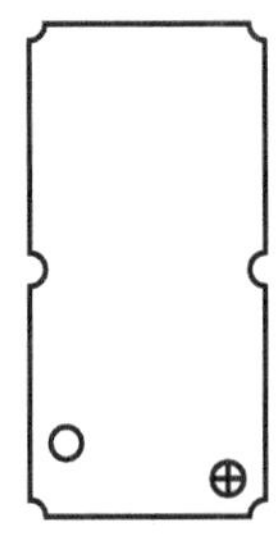
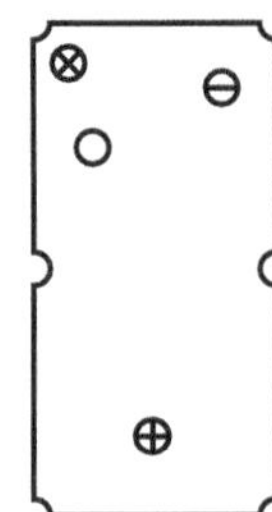
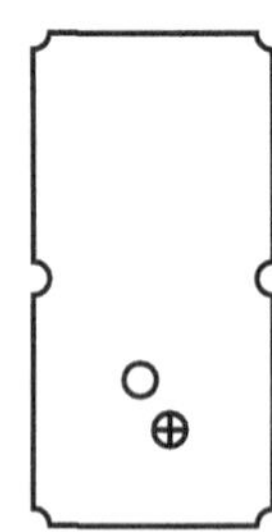
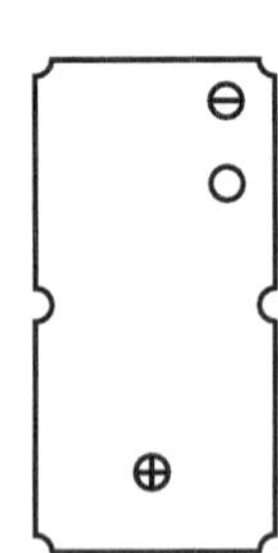

A ☐ B ☐ C ☐ D ☐ E ☐

Section 3 - Non Verbal Reasoning

In the questions below, the five figures can be rearranged to form a logical sequence.
Select the alternative that would most logically and simply be in the middle of the sequence.

Question 33

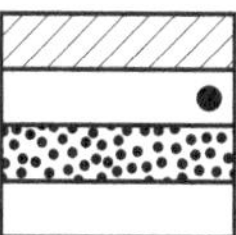 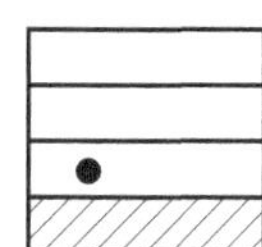 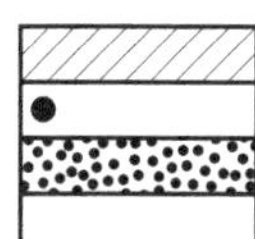 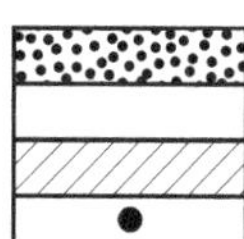 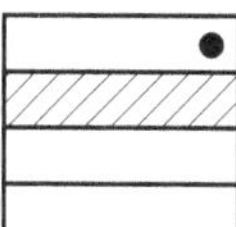

A ☐ B ☐ C ☐ D ☐ E ☐

Question 34

 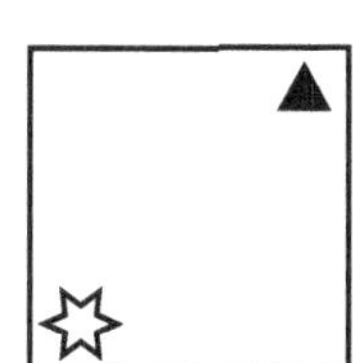 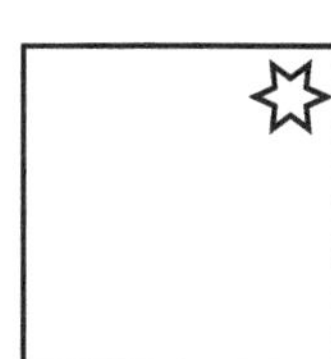 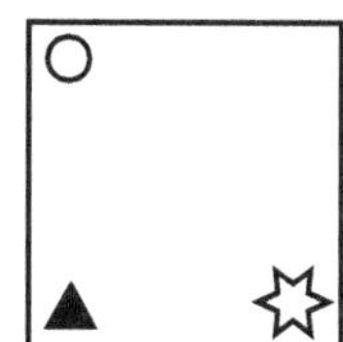 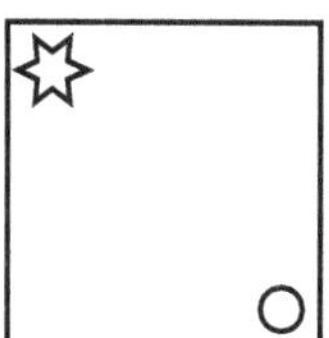

A ☐ B ☐ C ☐ D ☐ E ☐

Section 3 - Non Verbal Reasoning

In the questions below, the five figures can be rearranged to form a logical sequence. Select the alternative that would most logically and simply be in the middle of the sequence.

Question 35

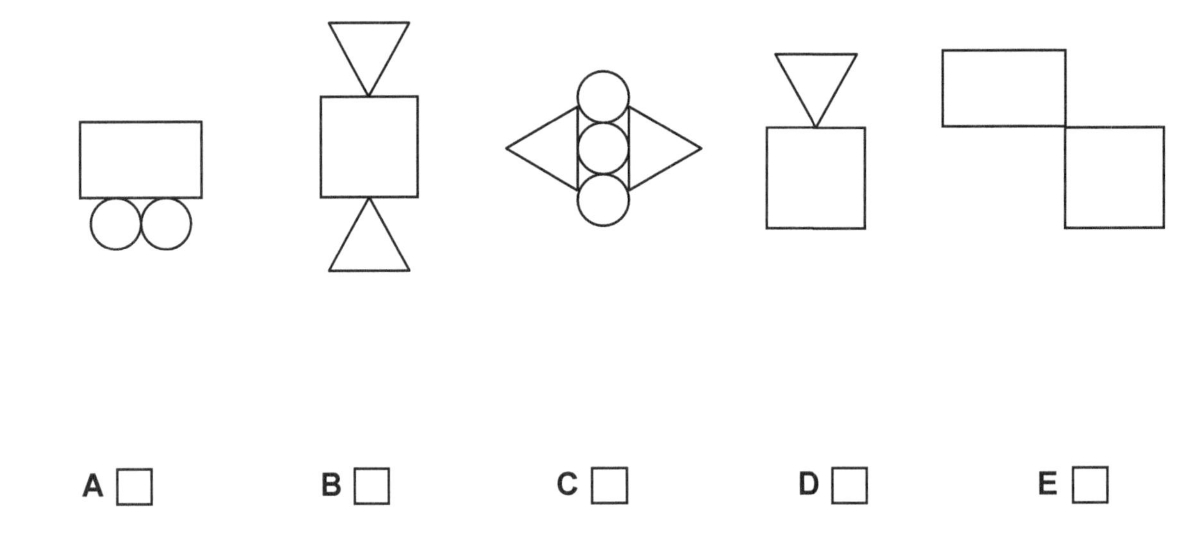

A ☐ B ☐ C ☐ D ☐ E ☐

Question 36

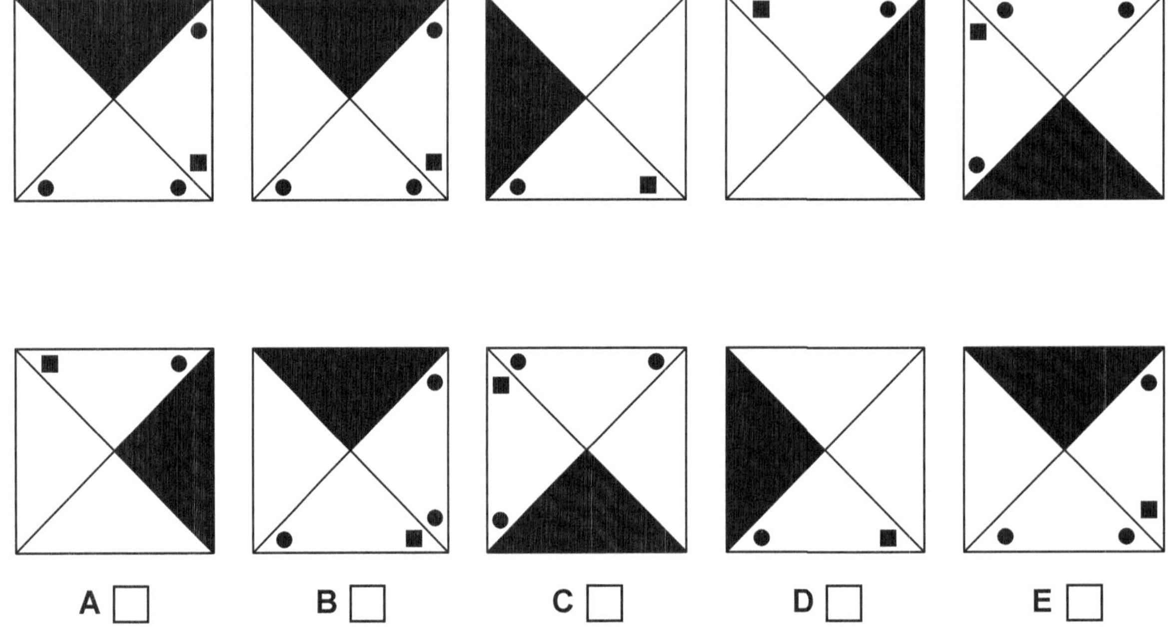

A ☐ B ☐ C ☐ D ☐ E ☐

Section 3 - Non Verbal Reasoning

In the questions below, the five figures can be rearranged to form a logical sequence. Select the alternative that would most logically and simply be in the middle of the sequence.

Question 37

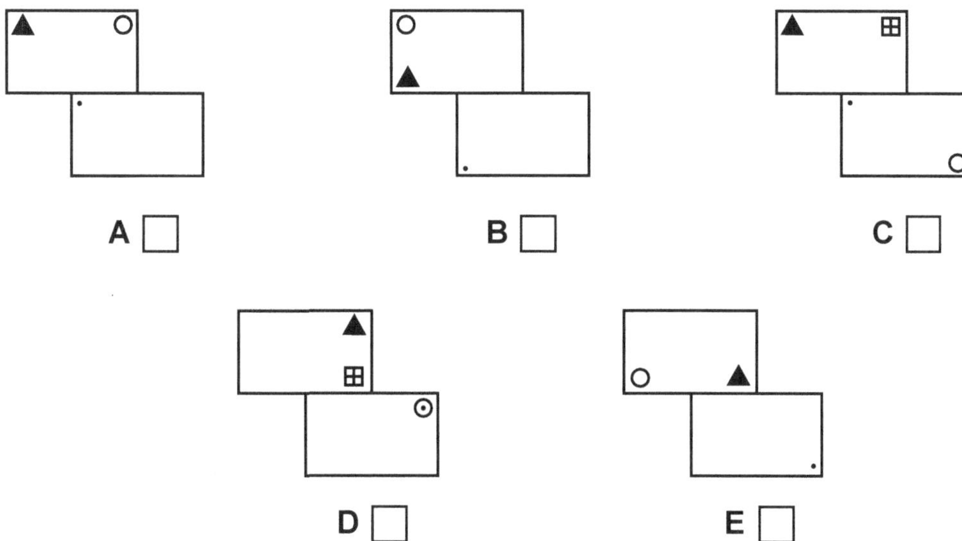

Question 38

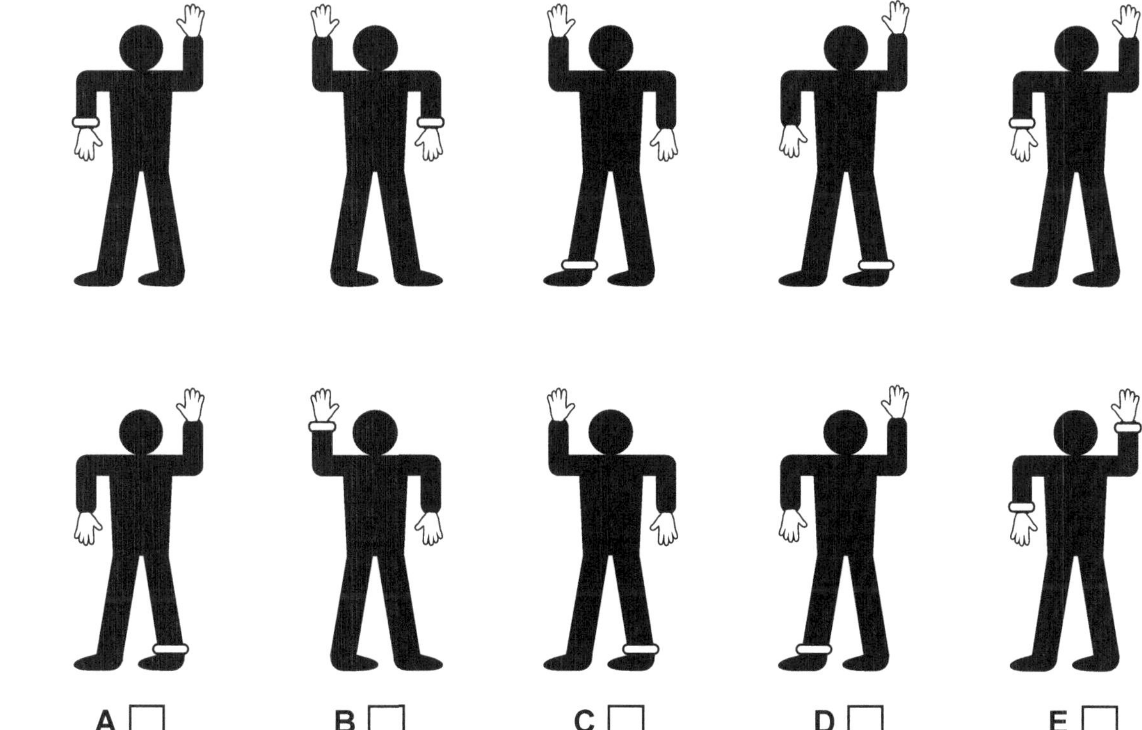

Section 3 - Non Verbal Reasoning

In the questions below, the five figures can be rearranged to form a logical sequence.
Select the alternative that would most logically and simply be in the middle of the sequence.

Question 39

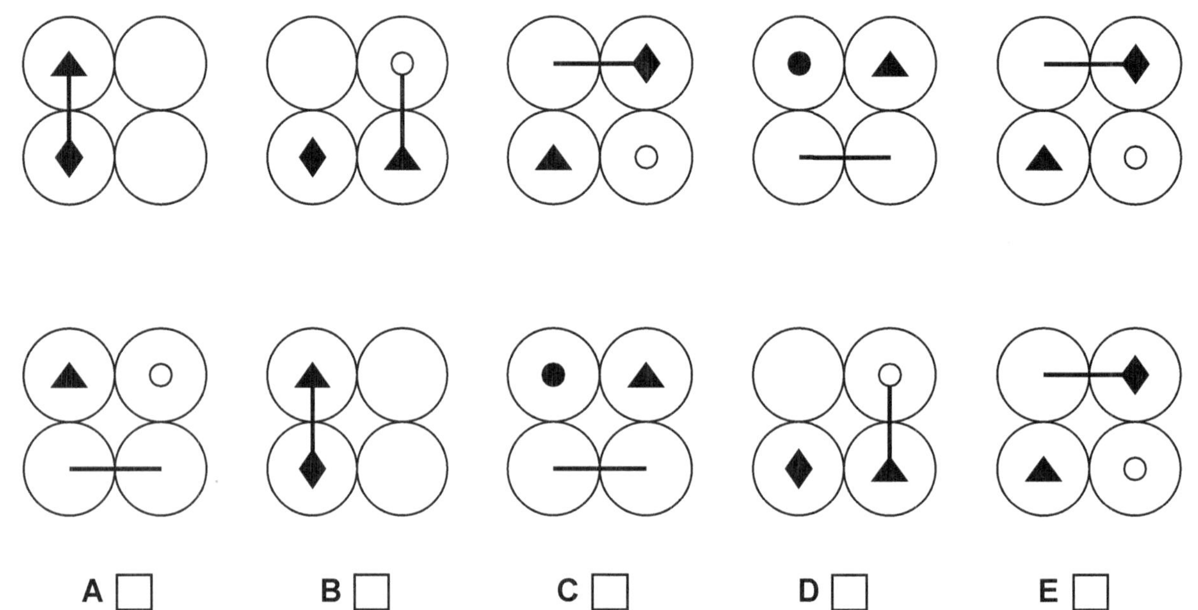

A ☐ B ☐ C ☐ D ☐ E ☐

Question 40

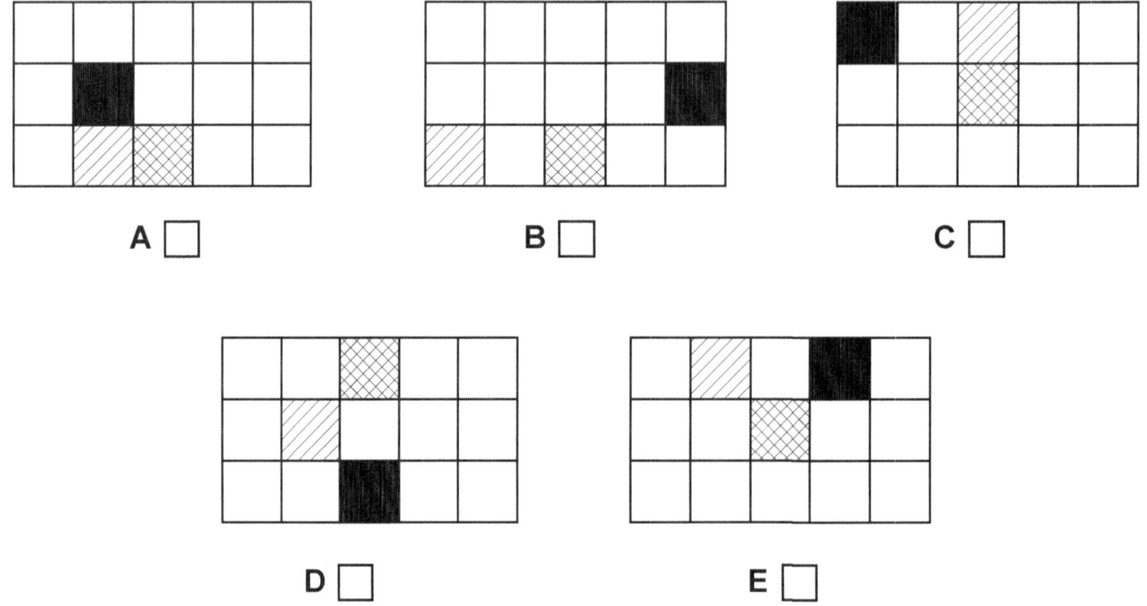

A ☐ B ☐ C ☐ D ☐ E ☐

Section 3 - Non Verbal Reasoning

In the questions below, the five figures can be rearranged to form a logical sequence.
Select the alternative that would most logically and simply be in the middle of the sequence.

Question 41

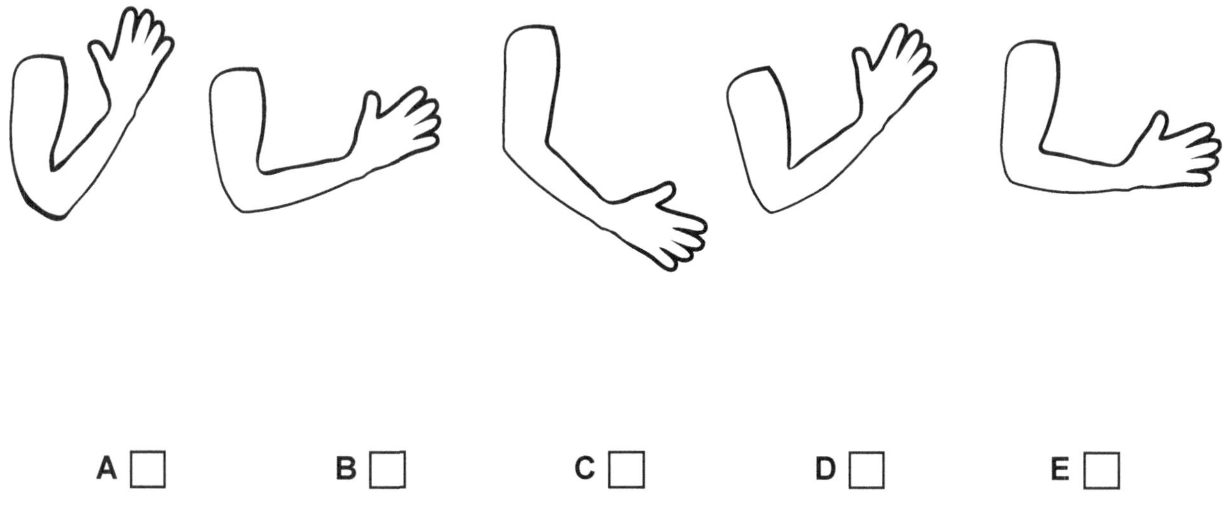

A ☐ B ☐ C ☐ D ☐ E ☐

Section 3 - Non Verbal Reasoning

In the questions below, the five figures can be rearranged to form a logical sequence. Select the alternative that would most logically and simply be in the middle of the sequence.

Question 42

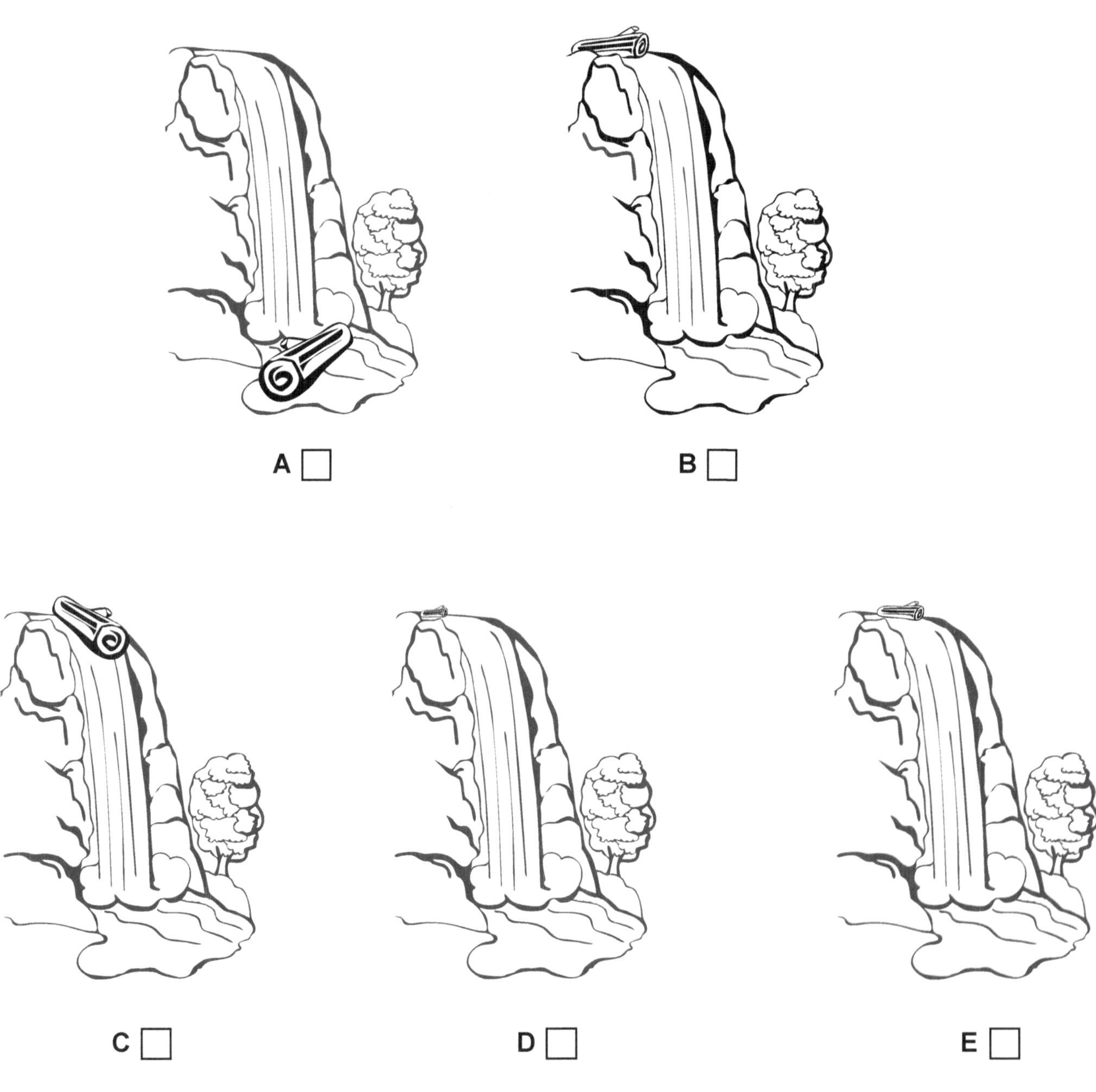

ANSWERS

Summary & Worked Solutions
Multiple Choice Answer Sheet

Section 3 Non-verbal Reasoning Answers

Summary of Answers

Question 1	A	Question 12	C	Question 23	A	Question 34	D
Question 2	E	Question 13	D	Question 24	B	Question 35	E
Question 3	C	Question 14	E	Question 25	E	Question 36	E
Question 4	E	Question 15	B	Question 26	C	Question 37	E
Question 5	C	Question 16	D	Question 27	A	Question 38	A
Question 6	A	Question 17	B	Question 28	D	Question 39	C
Question 7	D	Question 18	A	Question 29	D	Question 40	D
Question 8	B	Question 19	B	Question 30	A	Question 41	B
Question 9	E	Question 20	D	Question 31	A	Question 42	B
Question 10	A	Question 21	C	Question 32	A		
Question 11	B	Question 22	E	Question 33	D		

Answers with fully worked solutions

Note:

Questions 1 – 14 involve test-takers selecting the alternative that most logically continues the series.

Questions 15 – 28 involve test-takers completing the picture.

Questions 29 – 42 involve test-takers placing five pictures into a logical sequence and then selecting the middle picture from the correct sequence.

Question 1

A

The blocks are halving in size for the first three sequences and then doubling in size. Hence A is correct.

Question 2

E

There are several patterns within the successive squares. The top left hand number is halving each time thus in the answer box it must be a 1. The stars are increasing once on every second occasion, hence in the answer box there must be 6 stars in the right hand corner. Along the base the sum of the number of circles and the actual number is as follows: 26, 22, 19, 17 or decreasing by a decreasing rate of one each time. Thus the sum of the number of circles and the number in the answer box must be 16 – hence E is correct.

Question 3

C

There are two alternating patterns here: A becomes B and then becomes C. The middle letter goes backwards in the alphabet by one: Z, Y and then X. The third letter goes backwards by 4 letters, thus the final letter should be E. Hence C is correct.

Question 4

E

There are several competing patterns here. The black square moves clockwise in the following sequence: out and along 1, in and along 2, out and along 3, in and along 4. It is hidden in the 3rd picture by the circle. Thus the black square will be as shown in B and E.

The circle moves in a diagonal across and back and will be found in the position shown by B, C and E – but C has already been eliminated. The white triangle is in the same space in every answer and it thus not a discriminator.

The black triangle moves forward 1, back 2, forward 3, back 4 and thus would be found as shown in E, eliminating B.

Question 5

C

The whole triangle is moving anticlockwise, thus the black dot must be in the left hand lower corner. The actual arrow moves from the middle towards the corner and back to the middle – hence C is right.

Question 6

A

The black dot moves upwards and to the right making it disappear, thus the two dots at the top must disappear, so C can be eliminated. The top double lines move successive upwards one and would be second from the top as shown in A, D and E, thus B can be discounted. The lowest black double line moves up one space eliminating D.

This then means the answer is between A and E. E has two black dots. The middle dot cannot be justified thus A is the correct alternative.

Question 7

D

The first shape alternates being up and then mirror images downwards. Thus C and E are eliminated. The middle shape is rotating clockwise 90°, thus B is eliminated. The last shape (dot within circle) is rotating counter clockwise 90° and thus would be as shown in D (eliminating A).

Hence D is correct.

Question 8

B

Here the volume of water is halving and then doubling. Note the volume in D is one and half times that of the thin glass.

Question 9

E

The white dot moves clockwise one space at a time. The grey dot moves counter-clockwise two spaces at a time. The black dot moves clockwise three spaces at a time. When the white dot occupies the same space as another dot then it gets hidden. Thus, following these rules makes E correct.

Question 10

A

The middle line or lines are rotated 90° in successive patterns. The successive patterns are every second pattern. Thus the picture must look like it is at the start which is A.

Question 11

B

Tricky! Going around the outside, starting with the white square and moving anti-clockwise, each shape swaps with the shape in the middle of the box. Thus, the final picture must swap the inner black dot for the lower right-hand triangle, thus giving B.

Question 12

C

The colour or pattern sequences rotate through the following: grey to angled lines to dots to white to crosshatches back to grey and so on.

The only option that follows this sequence is C.

Question 13

D

Again, tricky! The pattern is based on 'powers' or indices. Thus in the first square look at the top two numbers. The first number is indexed by the second number. Thus 2^3 equals 8 – the number at the bottom of the square. Following this through we can see that 3^2 is 9, 3^3 is 27 and 2^4 is 16. The only answer that follows this pattern is $1^8 = 1$, thus D is correct.

Question 14

E

The first letter changes in successive boxes by a gap of 4 letters, then 8, then 12. Thus from B we have to go forward through the alphabet by a gap of 16 letters, giving us S. The second letter in the sequence moves forward by a gap of 6, then 10, then 14 (increasing also by 4 each time). Thus from J we go forward through the alphabet by 18 letters giving us C. Note the alphabet scrolls back to the start when we reach Z.

Question 15

B

Adding the shapes end-to-end gives B. Note, the left hand column indicates that the answer cannot be A.

Question 16

D

Wherever there are two digits below they add on the diagonal (going left to right) to give the number at the top. Thus 2 + 5 = 7, 3 + 5 = 8 and 4 + 0 = 4. There is no other pattern and the first two digits from the left are distractors.

Question 17

B

Very tricky! Look closely at the diagonals in any the groups of nine squares. You should notice that regardless of the shapes they move downwards and right in the next box of nine squares to the right.

Thus the answer must show this progression down and right. This is correctly done in B

Question 18

A

Feeling mathematical? The black shapes represent negative numbers and the white shapes represent positive numbers. The actual numbers are the number of sides of the shape – thus a circle is 1, a triangle 3, a square 4 and so forth. The instruction is given by the sign in the corners of each group of nine boxes.

So in the first box of nine in the top left hand corner a black circle (-1) + 4 (a white square) gives +3 (a white triangle in the inner box, top left-hand corner). Similarly, a square (4) minus a triangle (3) is a white circle (+1). When the calculation gives an answer of zero the inner boxes are empty.

The signs are true for multiplication, thus is the lower left-hand group of nine a black circle (-1) x a black circle (-1) gives +1 or a white circle.

Hence the missing box of four must be +3 (white triangle) minus –4 (black square) gives 3 + 4 = 7 (a heptagon). A black square times a black circle gives -4 x -1 = +4 or a white box. -1 (black circle) – 3 (white triangle) = -4 or black box. And a triangle plus a triangle is 3 + 3, which is 6 or a hexagon.

Thus the correct answer is A.

Question 19

B

Add the shapes right to left and remove overlapping lines and dots!

Question 20

D

The shapes move either clockwise or anti-clockwise across the rows. When the squiggly line occupies the same space as another shape the other shape is hidden.

Thus in the bottom row, the circle is moving anti-clockwise one space at a time, the star is moving clockwise one space and the squiggly line is moving anti-clockwise one space. Hence D is correct.

Question 21

C

The black dot on the right moves left three spaces at a time and the black dot on the left moves leftwards two spaces at a time. Following this pattern shows that they overlap in the third picture. Be careful to note which is moving 3 spaces and which is moving 2 spaces.

Question 22

E

There are five coloured triangles out of a total of eight. Thus only E shows the correct number of triangles coloured.

Question 23

A

The thinnest hand (the second hand) is moving 90° clockwise, but is covered in nearly every picture. The hour hand is alternating colour between black and white and is moving anti-clockwise 90° – in the last picture it is hidden by the minute hand.

The minute hand is moving clockwise three successive lots of 135° and then back 135°.

Question 24

B

Here each lot of 3 x 3 squares is adding from left to right. However, the black dots are moving counter-clockwise one space at a time and the crosshatch dots are moving clockwise one space at a time within the 9-box frame. Thus in the missing box the black dots at the top must move left one space each, whilst the lower dots must move right. The crosshatched dots must move clockwise by one space each too, hence B is correct.

Question 25

E

Here there is a large and small version of each shape in each row of 3 thus the missing shapes in the second row are a large square, a small square and a large circle as shown in E.

Question 26

C

The shapes are adding downwards in their column with overlapping lines, except outside lines, disappearing.

Question 27

A

Here the outside dots represent positive numbers and the inside dots represent negative numbers. The numbers are then added across the rows from left to right. Thus, in the first row -4 + 2 = -2.

In the second row +1 – 3 = -2. This means that in the third row -3 -1 = -4, hence A is correct. Note, C is also minus 4 but the orientation of the rectangle is incorrect.

Question 28

D

The triangles are adding from left to right and the sum is added to the next triangle and so forth. But, any overlapping lines disappear in the process. Thus, in the missing triangle there must be two parallel lines as in the far right top triangle these lines are missing. Similarly, the figure must also have a cross because the final figure has a cross and there is nothing in the middle figure to negate this.

Question 29

D

In each successive group of letters ONE letter changes. Hence the sequence must be:

OQUUA – PQUUA – PQUVA – PQUVB – PQBVB - thus the middle arrangement is PQUVA.

Question 30

A

The X does not move. The ball falls towards the middle of the circle from the top of the circle and the arrow moves in a diagonal line across through the middle of the circle, starting between the 7 and 8 on the clockface (225°).

Question 31

A

This sequence starts with 3 black diamonds and one white diamond. It then losses a black diamond on each successive picture until there are only white diamonds. The white diamonds then begin to change into black circles. The lines through the picture are alternately lost and restored.

Question 32

A

This is a game of billiards or pool where the white ball is the one striking the others and moving them into the pockets or shifting their position. Assuming the white ball is moving northwards in C then it would strike the crossed ball into the top left hand pocket. The white ball would then deflect rightwards and head toward the ball with the minus sign – at E. As it glances the minus ball that ball would head towards the top right pocket and the white ball would also deflect to strike the side of the table but in a trajectory closer to the middle of the right side pocket as shown in A.

The white ball would then continue down the table, striking the ball with the plus (at D) making the final position that shown in B.

Hence the middle of this sequence is A.

Question 33

D

The starting position is shown in figure C. From here the angled lines bar moves upwards, scrolling to the bottom and travelling one bar upwards at a time. The black dot is moving left to right but is also falling downwards by one row at a time, also scrolling to the top when it reaches the bottom. The pebbly row moves downwards one space at a time but will be obscured by the bar with the angled lines. Hence the sequence is C – B – D – E – A and the correct middle picture is D.

Question 34

D

The star is moving clockwise one space at a time. The black triangle alternates between the top right hand corner and the bottom left hand corner but whenever another shape occupies the same spot it is hidden. The circle is moving counter clockwise one space at a time. Hence the middle picture is D.

Question 35

E

Here the sum of the lines forms a numerical sequence. Thus a circle has a value of 1, a triangle3, a square and rectangle 4 each. Hence the picture in A equates to a 6 (2 circles and one square), the picture in B is worth 10 (2 triangles worth 3 and one square worth 4) and so on. The numerical sequence is 6 – 7 – 8 – 9 – 10 and the middle picture with 8 lines is the two boxes in E.

Question 36

E

The black triangle starts at the top and moves one space at a time counter clockwise. The triangle with the black dots moves clockwise on space at a time but can be obscured by the black triangle. The triangle with the square and dot also moves clockwise one space at a time and the black dot and the black square in the triangle switch places on each movement.

Question 37

E

The black triangle in the upper rectangle is moving counter clockwise one space at a time. The circle is doing the same but jumps down to the next rectangle (top right corner) on the fourth picture. The circle then continues but this time in a clockwise direction in the lower rectangle. The black dot in the lower rectangle is moving clockwise around that rectangle. When the circle jumps a new shape appears in the top box and it starts to move clockwise behind the black triangle.

This means that the sequence is A – B – E – D – C and thus E is correctly the middle picture.

Question 38

A

Careful eyes are required as there are several things occurring here. The wrist band is moving from the left wrist to the right wrist to the right ankle to the left ankle to the left wrist. The hands are alternatively moving up and down thus in the middle picture the writ band must be on the right ankle and the hands must be as they were – which is shown in A.

Question 39

C

Here the black triangle is moving clockwise one space at a time. The black line is also moving one position at a time, but it is moving counter-clockwise. The small white circle is moving clockwise, one space at a time, but when it overlaps with another shape it is hidden. Finally, the black diamond moves to the alternating corners (top right, bottom left) and gets hidden when the triangle occupies the same spot.

Question 40

D

The black square is falling downwards by one row and moving from left to right one space in successive pictures, scrolling to the top after it reaches the bottom. The square with the diagonal lines is moving upwards one space at a time but one it reaches the top of the column it moves to the left one space as it scrolls. The square with the crosshatches moves downwards to the bottom and then scrolls to the top, moving one space at a time and always staying in the middle column. Thus the sequence is: C – A – D – E – B and the correct middle picture is D.

Question 41

B

The arm is straightening and thus is moves in the following sequence: A – D – B – E – C. Thus the middle picture is B.

Question 42

B

This question shows a time sequence with the water pushing the log over the waterfall. Following the pictures shows that the correct order would be: D – E – B – C – A, thus giving the middle picture in order as B.

Notes

Notes

Notes

Notes

Notes

Notes

Essential Preparation for

UMAT

UNDERGRADUATE MEDICINE & HEALTH SCIENCES ADMISSION TEST

MULTIPLE CHOICE ANSWER SHEET

Use pencil when filling out this sheet

Fill in the circle correctly				
●	(B)	(C)	(D)	(E)

If you make a mistake neatly cross it out and circle the correct response				
⊗	●	(C)	(D)	(E)

1	(A)	(B)	(C)	(D)	(E)	22	(A)	(B)	(C)	(D)	(E)
2	(A)	(B)	(C)	(D)	(E)	23	(A)	(B)	(C)	(D)	(E)
3	(A)	(B)	(C)	(D)	(E)	24	(A)	(B)	(C)	(D)	(E)
4	(A)	(B)	(C)	(D)	(E)	25	(A)	(B)	(C)	(D)	(E)
5	(A)	(B)	(C)	(D)	(E)	26	(A)	(B)	(C)	(D)	(E)
6	(A)	(B)	(C)	(D)	(E)	27	(A)	(B)	(C)	(D)	(E)
7	(A)	(B)	(C)	(D)	(E)	28	(A)	(B)	(C)	(D)	(E)
8	(A)	(B)	(C)	(D)	(E)	29	(A)	(B)	(C)	(D)	(E)
9	(A)	(B)	(C)	(D)	(E)	30	(A)	(B)	(C)	(D)	(E)
10	(A)	(B)	(C)	(D)	(E)	31	(A)	(B)	(C)	(D)	(E)
11	(A)	(B)	(C)	(D)	(E)	32	(A)	(B)	(C)	(D)	(E)
12	(A)	(B)	(C)	(D)	(E)	33	(A)	(B)	(C)	(D)	(E)
13	(A)	(B)	(C)	(D)	(E)	34	(A)	(B)	(C)	(D)	(E)
14	(A)	(B)	(C)	(D)	(E)	35	(A)	(B)	(C)	(D)	(E)
15	(A)	(B)	(C)	(D)	(E)	36	(A)	(B)	(C)	(D)	(E)
16	(A)	(B)	(C)	(D)	(E)	37	(A)	(B)	(C)	(D)	(E)
17	(A)	(B)	(C)	(D)	(E)	38	(A)	(B)	(C)	(D)	(E)
18	(A)	(B)	(C)	(D)	(E)	39	(A)	(B)	(C)	(D)	(E)
19	(A)	(B)	(C)	(D)	(E)	40	(A)	(B)	(C)	(D)	(E)
20	(A)	(B)	(C)	(D)	(E)	41	(A)	(B)	(C)	(D)	(E)
21	(A)	(B)	(C)	(D)	(E)	42	(A)	(B)	(C)	(D)	(E)

Essential Preparation for

UMAT

UNDERGRADUATE MEDICINE & HEALTH SCIENCES ADMISSION TEST

MULTIPLE CHOICE ANSWER SHEET

Use pencil when filling out this sheet

Fill in the circle correctly				
●	B	C	D	E

If you make a mistake neatly cross it out and circle the correct response

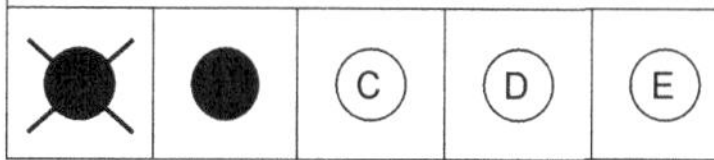

1	A	B	C	D	E	22	A	B	C	D	E
2	A	B	C	D	E	23	A	B	C	D	E
3	A	B	C	D	E	24	A	B	C	D	E
4	A	B	C	D	E	25	A	B	C	D	E
5	A	B	C	D	E	26	A	B	C	D	E
6	A	B	C	D	E	27	A	B	C	D	E
7	A	B	C	D	E	28	A	B	C	D	E
8	A	B	C	D	E	29	A	B	C	D	E
9	A	B	C	D	E	30	A	B	C	D	E
10	A	B	C	D	E	31	A	B	C	D	E
11	A	B	C	D	E	32	A	B	C	D	E
12	A	B	C	D	E	33	A	B	C	D	E
13	A	B	C	D	E	34	A	B	C	D	E
14	A	B	C	D	E	35	A	B	C	D	E
15	A	B	C	D	E	36	A	B	C	D	E
16	A	B	C	D	E	37	A	B	C	D	E
17	A	B	C	D	E	38	A	B	C	D	E
18	A	B	C	D	E	39	A	B	C	D	E
19	A	B	C	D	E	40	A	B	C	D	E
20	A	B	C	D	E	41	A	B	C	D	E
21	A	B	C	D	E	42	A	B	C	D	E

Essential Preparation for

UMAT

UNDERGRADUATE MEDICINE & HEALTH SCIENCES ADMISSION TEST

MULTIPLE CHOICE ANSWER SHEET

Use pencil when filling out this sheet

Fill in the circle correctly				
●	(B)	(C)	(D)	(E)

If you make a mistake neatly cross it out and circle the correct response				
⊗	●	(C)	(D)	(E)

1	(A)	(B)	(C)	(D)	(E)	22	(A)	(B)	(C)	(D)	(E)
2	(A)	(B)	(C)	(D)	(E)	23	(A)	(B)	(C)	(D)	(E)
3	(A)	(B)	(C)	(D)	(E)	24	(A)	(B)	(C)	(D)	(E)
4	(A)	(B)	(C)	(D)	(E)	25	(A)	(B)	(C)	(D)	(E)
5	(A)	(B)	(C)	(D)	(E)	26	(A)	(B)	(C)	(D)	(E)
6	(A)	(B)	(C)	(D)	(E)	27	(A)	(B)	(C)	(D)	(E)
7	(A)	(B)	(C)	(D)	(E)	28	(A)	(B)	(C)	(D)	(E)
8	(A)	(B)	(C)	(D)	(E)	29	(A)	(B)	(C)	(D)	(E)
9	(A)	(B)	(C)	(D)	(E)	30	(A)	(B)	(C)	(D)	(E)
10	(A)	(B)	(C)	(D)	(E)	31	(A)	(B)	(C)	(D)	(E)
11	(A)	(B)	(C)	(D)	(E)	32	(A)	(B)	(C)	(D)	(E)
12	(A)	(B)	(C)	(D)	(E)	33	(A)	(B)	(C)	(D)	(E)
13	(A)	(B)	(C)	(D)	(E)	34	(A)	(B)	(C)	(D)	(E)
14	(A)	(B)	(C)	(D)	(E)	35	(A)	(B)	(C)	(D)	(E)
15	(A)	(B)	(C)	(D)	(E)	36	(A)	(B)	(C)	(D)	(E)
16	(A)	(B)	(C)	(D)	(E)	37	(A)	(B)	(C)	(D)	(E)
17	(A)	(B)	(C)	(D)	(E)	38	(A)	(B)	(C)	(D)	(E)
18	(A)	(B)	(C)	(D)	(E)	39	(A)	(B)	(C)	(D)	(E)
19	(A)	(B)	(C)	(D)	(E)	40	(A)	(B)	(C)	(D)	(E)
20	(A)	(B)	(C)	(D)	(E)	41	(A)	(B)	(C)	(D)	(E)
21	(A)	(B)	(C)	(D)	(E)	42	(A)	(B)	(C)	(D)	(E)